GOLF CONNECTIONS

# A GOLF VACATION DIRECTORY

1992/93

## GOLF VACATION DESTINATIONS

in

ATLANTIC CANADA
EASTERN & SOUTH EASTERN U.S.A.

and

ISLAND GOLF

# KEY TO SYMBOLS

You may call ahead for starting tee times.

Practice driving area is available on site

Practice putting green is available on site

| | |
|---|---|
| $ | Low Green Fees: Up to $20.00 |
| $$ | Moderate Green Fees: $20.00 to $30.00 |
| $$$ | High Green Fees: Over $30.00 |

To play this course you must be invited by a member.

---



**3455 Harvester Rd. Unit #2, Burlington, Ontario L7N 3P2**
**Tel: (416)333-0019 Fax: (416)333-6883**



Data in this edition has been provided directly by the facilities, as of the end of December 1991. While every effort has been made to report their information accurately, we assume no responsibility for the information supplied by the individuals contacted or for any changes that have occured since our last contact with them.

If any of our readers find omissions or incorrect data in any of the listings we would appreciate being advised. We do however reserve the right to include and/or omit any entry by the facility, company, organization or individual which, in our judgement is not consistant with the objectives of GOLF CONNECTIONS.

We are grateful to many friends and associates who have provided input, assistance, and support. We encourage all our readers to use our advertisers' facilities, services, and/or products. Without their contributions, the purchase price of this Directory to you would be considerably higher.

## TABLE OF CONTENTS

GOLF CONNECTIONS

PUBLISHER
**Robert Thorpe**

PRODUCTION ASSISTANT
**Darlene Benny**

CREATIVE ARTIST
**Janet Thorpe**

EDITING
**Ken Elliot**

CARTOONS
**Al Konetzni**

GRAPHICS
**Ward Graphics**

---

PRESIDENT
**Robert Thorpe**

V.P. SALES & ADVERTISING
**Kathy Thorpe**

SR. ACCOUNT EXECUTIVE
**Mary Lou Totty**

ACCOUNT EXECUTIVES
**Lillian Stone**
**Gerri Hughes**

TELEMARKETING
**Craig Russell**

RESEARCH
**Judy Pauker**

**SECTION** **PAGE**



---

*"Taxes are just like golf - you drive your heart out to get to the green and then end up in the hole"* UNKNOWN

# SWING THROUGH CANADA WITH . . .

SERVING THE GOLF COMMUNITY

**TORONTO**
METRO TORONTO CONVENTION CENTRE
FEBRUARY 25 - 28,1993

**MONTREAL**
MONTREAL CONVENTION CENTRE
MARCH 5 - 7,1993

**VANCOUVER**
B.C. PLACE STADIUM
MARCH 26 - 28,1993

***ATTENTION U.S. RESORTS and GOLF DESTINATIONS !!!***

- Grow with the largest consumer golf shows in North America.
- THE CANADIAN PRO-AM GOLF SHOWS offer you a market you can't afford to miss.
- Canadian Golfers travel further, stay longer . . . and spend more money !
- Montreal, Toronto and Vancouver are the three largest golf markets in Canada.
- Over 75,000 eager golfers will attend our golfshows . . . be there to book vacations at your resort.
- Fill your hotel rooms and golf courses during the fall and winter months

**FOR EXHIBITOR & SPONSORSHIP INFORMATION CALL**
**CLAUDIO DEMARCHI at (416) 691-2852**

## COMING SOON - NEXT EDITION - Alabama

# THE ROBERT TRENT JONES GOLF TRAIL

*A trail of golf complexes is currently under construction that reaches from North Alabama to the sunny Gulf Coast.*

*The trail presently involves seven separate golf complexes - four 54-hole complexes located in Birmingham, Mobile, Huntsville and Auburn/Opelika, and three 36-hole complexes in Dothan, Greenville and Anniston/Gadsden.*

*Named after world reknowned golf course architect Robert Trent Jones, who has designed what is certainly the finest collection of public golf courses in the world, the complexes on "the trail" will open the courses at various times throughout 1992 and early 1993 as they are completed.*

*Exceptional in quality and affordable in price. Watch for more on the ROBERT TRENT JONES GOLF TRAIL in our next edition.*

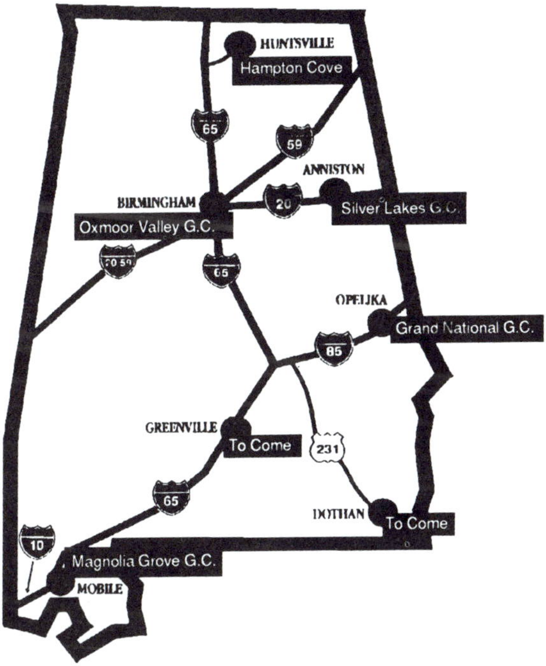


FOR MORE INFORMATION CONTACT:

SUNBELT GOLF

SunBelt Golf Corporation
100 SunBelt Parkway
Birmingham, AL 35211

**Tel: (205)942-1177 • Fax: (205)942-7080**

# COMING SOON - NEXT EDITION - Arizona

*The Great Desert Discovery*

**Francisco Grande**
RESORT & GOLF CLUB

## FRANCISCO GRANDE RESORT & GOLF CLUB

**CASA GRANDE, AZ (4 mi. West of city of Casa Grande, between Phoenix & Tucson)**
Telephone: (602)836-6444 Toll Free: 1-800-237-4238

Gen. Mgr.: William J. Deskus
Head Pro: Kent Chase
Course Supt.: Tom O'Leary
Architect: Ralph M. Plummer

18 - R - 6975 - 72

A well maintained golf course in the Heart of the Great Southwest. Tree lined fairways and bent grass greens. "Arizona's Friendliest Resort".

| | |
|---|---|
| $$$ | Resort |
| Golf Pkgs. | Public |
| Power Carts | Lessons |
| Lounge | Snack Bar |
| Meals | Open All Year |

**Tournament Players Club**
TPC
STARPASS

## TOURNAMENT PLAYERS CLUB AT STARPASS

**TUCSON, AZ (3-1/2 mi. west from 22nd. St. exit off Interstate 10)**
Telephone: (602)622-6060 Fax: (602)624-1445

Gen. Mgr./Dir. of Golf: Bill Grove
Head Pro: Bob Janes
Course Supt.: Don Weingartner
Architect: Robert Cupp

18 - R - 6300 - 72

Features the beauty of the Tucson Mountains and Sonoran Desert. Rated in the Top 10 by GOLF DIGEST.Home of the *PGA Tour Northern Telecom Open.*

| | |
|---|---|
| $$$ | |
| Golf Pkgs. | Public |
| Power Carts | Lessons |
| Lounge | Snack Bar |
| Meals | Open All Year |

8 Championship
Golf Courses

# Comfort Inn

## Gold Coast

**Open
All Year**

- 112th St. & Coastal Hwy.
- Adjoins Gold Coast Mall
- Jacuzzi Rooms
- Microwave, Refrigerator & Wet Bar in all Rooms
- 24-Hour Convenience Store
- Libby's Restaurant & Lounge
- Meeting & Banquet Facilities
- Enclosed Heated Pool & Jacuzzi
- Gold Hospitality Award Winner
- Golf Packages

**Best Rates In Ocean City!**

11201 Coastal Highway, Ocean City, MD 21842
(410) 524-3000 or Toll Free: **(800) 221-2222**

DRIVE CAREFULLY
Entering . . .
GOLF VACATIONLAND
. . . Swing Easy, Enjoy !!!

GOLF CONNECTIONS

# ATLANTIC CANADA

Pages 9-32

Mill River, P.E.I.

# We invite you to break
# gulf view par five, thir

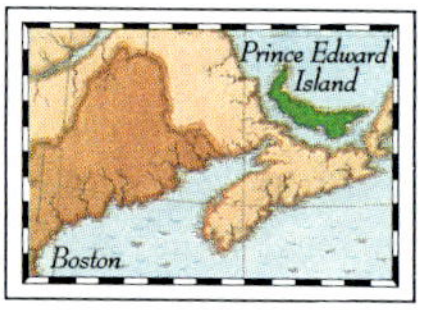


It fools you. Maybe it's the blue of the ocean you can see just beyond the green that distracts—but this third hole is one to cry about. You can play it smart. You can play it aggressive. For sure you're going to have to play it very carefully.

Our value vacation golf packages have opened the door to one of Prince Edward Island's best kept secrets. We are a golfer's paradise.

Green Gables is just one of twelve courses spotted throughout the island. Other courses that'll win your respect and have you ask the pro to check your swing include the Mill River Resort and the Brudenell River Resort course where the Atlantic Classic is played.

Play the island: Belvedere Golf Course • Brudenell River Golf Course • Clyde River Golf Course • Glen Afton C
• Stanhope Golf Course • Summerside G

# ›ur heart at the 530 yard, hole at Green Gables.

We've got eight eighteen-hole courses and four nines on the island. And, they're not all mean. All the courses are within easy driving distance wherever you are on the island. You can get on the green anywhere, play through and still make it in time to enjoy one of our great beaches.

This year, swing our way. You can fly, drive or cruise to Prince Edward Island to enjoy the best golf of your life. Ask your travel agent about value vacation packages to one of the world's great islands. **For more information Dial the Island, 1-800-565-0267, Operator 11.** Or write Department of Tourism and Parks, P.O. Box 940, Dept. 11, Charlottetown, Prince Edward Island, Canada, C1A 7M5.

PRINCE EDWARD ISLAND CANADA ®
*One of the world's great islands*

e • Green Gables Golf Course • Forest Hills Golf Course • Mill River Golf Course • Rustico Resort Golf Course
• (Lakeside Golf Course—Open June, 1993).

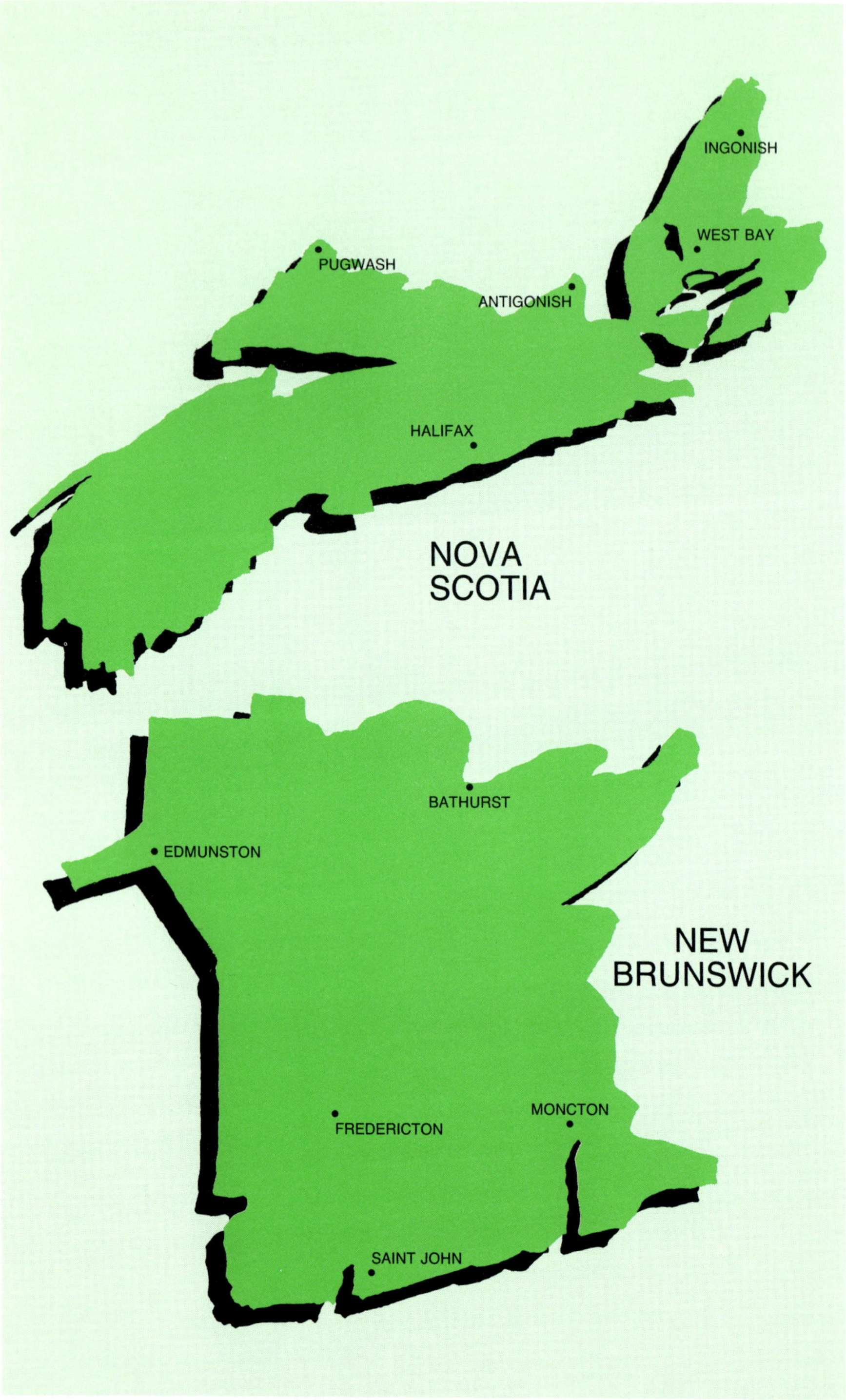
INGONISH
WEST BAY
PUGWASH
ANTIGONISH
HALIFAX
NOVA SCOTIA
BATHURST
EDMUNSTON
NEW BRUNSWICK
FREDERICTON
MONCTON
SAINT JOHN

1992/93 DIRECTORY

# Golf Vacations

## ATLANTIC CANADA

Pages 9-32

GOLF CONNECTIONS

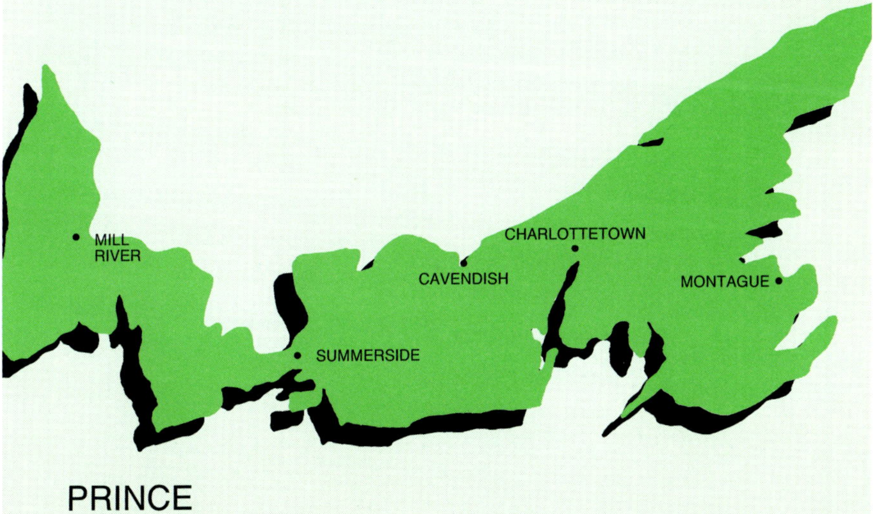


PRINCE EDWARD ISLAND

## BELVEDERE GOLF & WINTER CLUB INC.

**CHARLOTTETOWN, P.E.I. (On Greensview Dr., just S. of Peters Rd.)**
**Telephone: (902)566-5542**

Manager: James Smith
Head Pro: Cecil Dowling
Course Supt.: Nancy Pierce

18 - R - 6372 - 72

| | |
|---|---|
| $$ | |
| | Public |
| Power Carts | Lessons |
| Lounge | Snack Bar |
| Meals | |

A challenging 18 hole course with a diversity of greens and demanding fairways. Five minutes from downtown Charlottetown and excellent accommodations, it offers convenient pleasure for the golfer.

PROVINCIAL
PARKS
PRINCE EDWARD ISLAND, CANADA
*Naturally Entertaining!*

## BRUDENELL RIVER PROVINCIAL GOLF COURSE

**MONTAGUE, P.E.I. (On Route #3, 32 Mi. E. of Charlottetown)**
**Telephone: (902)652-2356**

Manager: Jack Kane
Head Pro: Ron Giggey
Course Supt.: Dale Murchison
Architect: C.E. "Robbie" Robinson

18 - R - 6000 - 72

Rated #19 in Canada by Score Magazine this course is the site of four National Amatuer Golf Championship and four Canadian Tour stops.

| | |
|---|---|
| $ | |
| Golf Pkgs. | Public |
| Power Carts | Lessons |
| Lounge | Snack Bar |
| Meals | |

## CLYDE RIVER GOLF CLUB

**CLYDE RIVER, P.E.I. (8 Mi. from Charlottetown, 1 Mi. off the Trans-Canada Hwy.)**
**Telephone: (902)675-2585 Off Season: (902)675-4602**

Manager: Oswald MacEachern
Course Supt.: Roger Cassey

9 - R - 3156 - 36

A gently rolling course set amidst a rural agricultural area.

| | |
|---|---|
| $ | |
| | Public |
| Power Carts | |
| | Snack Bar |
| | |

**FOREST HILLS GOLF COURSE**

## FOREST HILLS GOLF COURSE

**CAVENDISH, P.E.I. (On Route 6, the north shore, across from Rainbow Valley)**
**Telephone: (902)963-2357**

Owner: Eleanor Rowledge

9 - R - 2800 - 36

These are among the most challenging
9 holes of golf on Prince Edward Island.

| | |
|---|---|
| $ | |
| | Public |
| Power Carts | Lessons |
| | Snack Bar |
| | |

## GLEN AFTON GOLF COURSE

**NINE MILE CREEK, P.E.I. (Follow Route 19 from Cornwall to Nine Mile Creek.)**
**Telephone: (902)675-3000**

Owner: Delmar Currie
Pro Shop Mgr.: Karen Currie
Course Supt.: Harley Currie
Architect: Bill Robinson

18 - R - 5736 - 70

A warm and friendly 18 hole golf course featuring gently rolling hills, sand traps, water hazards and woods, with many holes overlooking the beautiful Northumberland Strait.

| | |
|---|---|
| $ | |
| | Public |
| Power Carts | |
| | Snack Bar |
| | |

## GREEN GABLES GOLF COURSE

**CAVENDISH, P.E.I. (Located on Route #6)**
**Telephone: (902)963-2488**

Owner: Prince Edward Island National Park
Head Pro: Errol Nicholson - CPGA

18 - R - 6331 - 72
Rating: Men's - 70.5, Ladies' - 73

Each hole at this course has been named for a person or place
written of by Lucy Maude Montgomery in her tales of "Anne of Green Gables".

| | |
|---|---|
| $$ | |
| Golf Pkgs. | Public |
| Power Carts | Lessons |
| Lounge | Snack Bar |
| Meals | |

PROVINCIAL
PARKS
PRINCE EDWARD ISLAND, CANADA
Naturally Entertaining!

## MILL RIVER PROVINCIAL GOLF COURSE

**MILL RIVER, P.E.I. (Route 2 to Mill River)**
**Telephone: (902)859-2238 Fax: (902)859-2486**
**Office: (902)859-2448**

Manager: Greg McKee
Head Pro: Steve Dowling - CPGA
Course Supt.: Blair Duggan - CGSA
Architect: C.E. "Robbie" Robinson
18 - R - 6830 - 72

"Set among hills of spruce this course features one of the most unusual water holes anywhere. The 8th hole is split in two by a chain of small ponds running the entire length of the fairway, creating two narrow landing areas and a scary tee shot." *Golf Illustrated 1991*

| | |
|---|---|
| $ | Resort |
| Golf Pkgs. | Public |
| Power Carts | Lessons |
| Lounge | Snack Bar |
| Meals | |

S G C
SUMMERSIDE GOLF CLUB

## SUMMERSIDE GOLF CLUB

**SUMMERSIDE, P.E.I. (On Water Street in Summerside.)**
**Telephone: (902)436-2505 Office: (902)436-2246**

General Manager: Jerry Eman
Director of Golf: TerryHamilton - CPGA

18 - R - 6239 - 72

Home of the Lobster Carnival Open and the Atlantic Senior Open.

| | |
|---|---|
| $ | |
| | Public |
| Power Carts | Lessons |
| Lounge | Snack Bar |
| Meals | |

## RUSTICO RESORT GOLF & COUNTRY CLUB

**SOUTH RUSTICO, P.E.I. (At Rte. 242, off Rte. 6, 12 Mi. from Charlottetown.)**
**Telephone: (902)963-2357 Fax: (902)963-3205**

Manager: John Langdale
Head Pro: David Bowlan
Course Supt.: Mark Sheridan
Architects: J. Proud/J. Langdale

18 - R - 5900 - 72
All holes have a view of the ocean. This course is moderately wooded, adding to the challenge for the experienced golfer but not intimidating for the recreational golfer.

| | |
|---|---|
| $ | Resort |
| Golf Pkgs. | Public |
| Power Carts | Lessons |
| Lounge | Snack Bar |
| Meals | |

Imagine . . . a rolling patchwork of woods and fields, river and shore, hills and open sky . . . bobbing boats at a tiny village fishing wharf piled high with lobster traps and sea going gear . . . the special colours of an Island sunset, straight from an artist's palette, diffused over a darkening land. Savour these views for real at *WILD GOOSE LODGE*

## GOLF VACATION PACKAGES

We have designed our special two, three, and four day golf packages with your love of the game in mind. Four of the Island's most interesting and challenging golf courses have been selected for your enjoyment:

- GREEN GABLES GOLF COURSE -

- MILL RIVER GOLF COURSE -

- SUMMERSIDE GOLF CLUB -

- BRUDENELL GOLF COURSE -

*WILD GOOSE LODGE*, centrally located for travel to all four golf courses, offers comfortable private accommodation, as well as a common lounge area where you can swap your favorite "hole-in-one" stories with fellow golfers.

Your golf vacation package includes accommodation, green fees at your chosen golf course, daily breakfast, a dinner voucher, as well as three cooked market lobsters per golfer taking our three or four day golf package.

**LET US HELP YOU PLAN YOUR NEXT GOLFING VACATION**

For further information call or write:
Hughena or Jim Duggan - **Leisure Services Inc.**

**(902)886-2177**

French River, R.R. #2 Kensington, P.E.I. Canada C0B 1M0

DRIVE CAREFULLY
Thank you for visiting ...
PRINCE EDWARD ISLAND
... Come again soon

# DREAM GREENS

New Brunswick

# Great Value Golf Getaways

**ALL PACKAGES INCLUDE:**

• *Executive Accommodations (2 Nights)* • *Full Breakfast (2 Days)*
• *Green Fees (2 rounds)* • *Power Cart (2 rounds)* • *All Taxes*
(Advance Reservations Required - Minimum 7 Days. Subject to Availablitiy)

Canadian Pacific Hotels & Resorts

The Algonquin

from **$262.50** per person / double occ.

The Algonquin Resort
Reservations
St. Andrews, N.B. E0G 2X0

*Play on Algonquin's own 18 hole, 6546 yard, par 72 course where scenic hazards are abundant.*

Telephone: ***(506)529-8823*** • Facsimile: ***(506)529-4194***
New Brunswick Toll Free: ***1-800-268-9411***

KingsClear Hotel & Resort

from **$202.50** per person / double occ.

KingsClear Hotel & Resort
R.R. #6
Fredericton, N.B. E3B 4X7

*Play Mactaquac, a 6423 yard, 18 hole, par 72 Golf Course set in one of New Brunswick's beautiful parks.*

Telephone: ***(506)363-5111*** • Facsimile: ***(506)363-3000***
New Brunswick Toll Free: ***1-800-561-5111***

Best Western Independent Worldwide Lodging

Danny's Inn & Conference Centre

from **$177.50** per person / double occ.

Best Western Danny's Inn
&Conference Centre
P.O. Box #180
Bathhurst, N.B. E2A 3Z2

*Play Gowan Brae, the course that Score Magazine called the "Pebble Beach of New Brunswick". The 14th green is shown on our title page.*

Telephone: ***(506)546-6621*** • Facsimile: ***(506)548-3266***
North America Toll Free: ***1-800-528-1234***

Buy one of the New Brunswick golf packages in this publication and be eligible to win a 3 or 4 day golf vacation. For details inquire while booking.

New Brunswick
C · A · N · A · D · A

Canadian Pacific Hotels & Resorts

# The Algonquin

There's Gaelic magic for golfers everywhere in the word . . . St. Andrews. New Brunswick's St. Andrews, on the Bay of Fundy in the southwest part of Canada's gateway to the Atlantic provinces, lives up to the magic.

It's an historic, seaside resort town in the best tradition of Eastern seaboard resorts. Founded by United Empire Loyalists in 1783, more than half its buildings are over 100 years old. One of the most imposing buildings is the red-tile turreted Algonquin Resort built in 1914 as one of Canada's grand "railway hotels."

The Algonquin was named "Canada's Resort of the Year for 1991" and with good reason. Executive accommodations are enhanced by fine dining in an elegant room overlooking lawns, gardens, tennis courts and the swimming pool. The resort also features a health spa. The Library Lounge and the Dockside are relaxing watering spots after a busy day of golf - one of the most appealing features of the Algonquin.

People who have played both St. Andrews, Scotland and the Algonquin consider the Canadian course to have more hazards and a greater variety of shots. Thirteen of the holes are played near salt water and the seascapes and salt breezes make it a most enjoyable course.

St. Andrews' town wharf is a tee off spot for different kinds of outdoor activity. Whale watching, scenic cruises and deep sea diving can be booked. The sailing on Passamaquoddy Bay, with its incredible Fundy Tides, is challenging and invigorating.

St. Andrews is a popular destination, not only for golfers but for bird-watchers, hikers and naturalists, with the sea all around. The Huntsman Marine Science Centre and Sunbury Shores Arts and Nature Centre both offer a variety of workshops and courses in marine life study, arts, and crafts.

Buy one of the New Brunswick golf packages in this publication and be eligible to win a 3 or 4 day golf vacation. For details inquire while booking.

New Brunswick

C·A·N·A·D·A

# KINGSCLEAR
## HOTEL & RESORT

*Just minutes from the centre of New Brunswick's capital city, Fredericton, the scenic Saint John River becomes a huge lake as the river waters are held back by the Mactaquac Dam. This major hydroelectric generating facility has created a vast recreational area known as Mactaquac Country.*

*The centrepiece of the area is Mactaquac Provincial Park, a year round park featuring hiking trails, campsites, nature interpretation programs and a terrific, 18 hole championship golf course. This summer Mactaquac will be the only Atlantic Canada venue for a Canadian Professional Golf Association pro event . . . The Priority Courier Atlantic Classic, August 24-30.*

*Overlooking the Mactaquac headpond is one of New Brunswick's newest resorts. The KingsClear Hotel and Resort was developed by the Native community of the nearby Kingsclear Reserve and is managed by ATLIFIC Hotels and Resorts who offer hospitality from the Atlantic to the Pacific. Both executive suites and cottages ensure luxurious relaxation. The KingsClear Hotel and Resort caters particularly to the sportsman and woman who enjoy the thrill of smallmouth bass fishing and world class salmon angling, as well as great golf. After an active day, guests unwind in the indoor pool, whirlpool and exercise area and enjoy a leisurely meal watching the sun set on the Saint John River.*

*Fredericton itself offers more urban pursuits with live theatre, a fascinating museum housing, among other displays, an incredible 43 pound stuffed frog! The Beaverbrook Art Gallery is one of the country's finest, containing a large and interesting collection of Cornelius Kreighoff paintings, depicting outdoor scenes and activities, as well as Salvador Dali's famous Santiago el Grande.*

Buy one of the New Brunswick golf packages in this publication and be eligible to win a 3 or 4 day golf vacation. For details inquire while booking.

**New Brunswick**
C · A · N · A · D · A

*When the explorer Jacques Cartier came to northern New Brunswick in 1604, he named the waters he sailed "Baie des Chaleurs" - Bay of Warmth. Bathurst is nestled in the heart of the bay and its hospitality is as warm as the waters it overlooks.*

*With distinct French flare, the city was the site of an earlier settlement established by Nicolas Denys, the governor of Acadia. Today the downtown is a thriving shopping centre and features two farmers' markets where people congregate for conversation and fresh produce.*

*Miles of sandy beaches, magnificent scenery and fresh seafood lure visitors back to Bathurst again and again. Some come to try and glimpse the illusive "Phantom Ship", a ghostly apparition of a ship on fire, which many local people vow they have seen.*

*Some come to play Gowan Brae, one of the Maritimes' finest golf courses. SCORE, Canada's national golf magazine called Gowan Brae the "Pebble Beach of New Brunswick". Its 17th hole is probably one of the toughest par threes in the province - 241 yards usually played against the stiff breeze off the Bay. Then again, many players remember the 13th hole - par 4, 449 yards on the side of a hill. Gowan Brae's 14th green graces our colour title page.*

*A golfing vacation in Bathurst is enhanced by the executive accommodation of the Best Western Danny's Inn & Conference Centre. Danny's is a small, friendly and well-appointed resort with a heated pool, tennis and shuffle board courts and a nearby private beach. The restaurant is popular for its fine seafood and also features Lobster Cook-outs.*

*At the Bathurst Marina, visitors can book deepsea fishing excursions, board-sailing, scuba diving and cruises into the Bay to try to site the Phantom Ship.*

Buy one of the New Brunswick golf packages in this publication and be eligible to win a 3 or 4 day golf vacation. For details inquire while booking.

New Brunswick
C · A · N · A · D · A

# HOWARD JOHNSON®

*For the footloose traveller, with golf clubs in the trunk of the car and a few days to explore, there is a sweeping tour of New Brunswick that will relax and rejuvinate.*

*The tour takes in four cities around the province and in each the Howard Johnson provides executive accommodation with indoor pools and saunas, friendly restaurants and the excellent service that Howard Johnson guests expect and enjoy.*

*Starting in the northwest corner of Canada's gateway to the Atlantic provinces, Edmundston is the first stop. The capital of the mythical Republic of Madawaska, Edmundston is a small, cosmopolitan city whose French inhabitants appreciate good food and good times.*

*The Edmundston Golf Club is a scenic 18 hole championship course over rolling hills. It features a restaurant, a bar and an outdoor swimming pool. This summer Edmundston will host the New Brunswick Senior Men's Championship, August 3-6.*

*After Edmundston, the New Brunswick tour continues southward down the panoramic Saint John River Valley to Fredericton, the provincial capital. Throughout the downtown area, Fredericton's Victorian and Edwardian homes are shaded by a canopy of stately elms.*

*A special treat for golfers is the 18 hole championship Mactaquac Park Golf Club, the centrepiece of the Provincial Park. Just 20 minutes from downtown, the course overlooks the headpond of the Mactaquac Dam where smallmouth bass fishing is another popular sport.*

*From the Capital, the tour continues down the Saint John River to Canada's oldest incorporated city, Saint John - the Loyalist City and the province's major seaport.*

*The Hampton Country Club, just outside Saint John, is set in the serene hills overlooking the lower reaches of the Saint John River. The 6193-yard course features a long carry over water on the fifth hole and a 666-yard par 6 sixth hole.*

*The final stop takes the golfer to one of the province's most curious phenomena, Magnetic Hill, where vehicles appear to coast uphill without power. Located just next to the hill is the Magnetic Hill Golf & Country Club. A mixture of flat and hilly terrain,the course is challenging but golf balls only roll uphill with the assistance of a golf club.*

*The course is just minutes from downtown Moncton with its outstanding shopping and eclectic mix of tempting restaurants.*

*Throughout this New Brunswick tour, Howard Johnson pamper their guests with special golfing arrangements and evening relaxation in their welcoming lounges and restaurants.*

Buy one of the New Brunswick golf packages in this publication and be eligible to win a 3 or 4 day golf vacation. For details inquire while booking.

New Brunswick
C·A·N·A·D·A

# HOWARD JOHNSON®

**ALL PACKAGES INCLUDE:**
*• Executive Accommodations (2 Nights) • Full Breakfast (2 Days)*
*• Green Fees (2 Rounds) • Power Cart (2 Rounds) • All Taxes*
(Advance Reservations Required - Minimum 7 Days, Subject to availablility)

## Howard Johnson - Edmundston

from **$190.00** per person/ double occ.

*Play at Edmundston Golf Club, a beautiful, challenging course where over sixty five sand traps (with new sand) await you.*

Reservations: 100 Rice Street, Edmundston, N.B. E3V 1T4
Telephone: ***(506)739-7321*** • Facsimile: ***(506)735-9101***

## Howard Johnson - Fredericton

from **$182.50** per person/ double occ.

*Play at Mactaquac Park Golf Club one of Canada's great courses. Long wide fairways with deer crossings on most holes.*

Reservations: P.O. Box 1414, Lower St. Mary's
Trans-Canada Hwy. 2, Fredericton, N.B. E3B 5E3
Telephone: ***(506)472-0480*** • Facsimile: ***(506)472-0170***

## Howard Johnson - Saint John

from **$182.50** per person/ double occ.

*Play at Hampton Country Club set in serene hills overlooking the Saint John River. Has a unique 666 yard par 6 sixth hole.*

Reservations: 400 Main Street, Saint John, N.B. E2K 4N5
Telephone: ***(506)642-2622*** • Facsimile: ***(506)658-1529***

## Howard Johnson - Moncton

from **$185.00** per person/ double occ.

*Play at Magnetic Hill Golf & Country Club, a very picturesque course located next to World Famous Magnetic Hill.*

Reservations: Trans-Canada Hwy. at Magnetic Hill
P.O. Box 5005, Moncton, N.B. E1C 8R7
Telephone: ***(506)384-1050*** • Facsimile: ***(506)859-6070***

Buy one of the New Brunswick golf packages in this publication and be eligible to win a 3 or 4 day golf vacation. For details inquire while booking.

New Brunswick
C · A · N · A · D · A

## ALGONQUIN GOLF CLUB

**ST. ANDREWS, N.B. (On Reed Ave., three blocks from The Algonquin Resort)**
**Telephone: (506)529-8823** **N.B. Toll Free: 1-800-268-9411**
**Fax: (506)529-4194**

Manager: J.W. Frise
Head Pro: Lindon Garron
Course Supt.: Leon Harvey
Architect: Donald Ross

18 - R - 6546 - 72

This course offers a variety of scenic views, The Town of St. Andrews, the Harbour and the Bay. Accommodations available at the resort. For more information see our full page ad on page 27.

| | |
|---|---|
| $$ | Resort |
| Golf Pkgs. | Semi-Private |
| Power Carts | Lessons |
| Lounge | Snack Bar |
| Meals | |

## EDMUNDSTON GOLF CLUB

**EDMUNDSTON, N.B. ( On Victoria St., 2.5 Km from City Bridge, off Church St.)**
**Telephone: (506)735-5667** **Other: (506)735-3086**
**Fax: (506)739-6960**

Manager: Ed Dunn
Head Pro: Ed Dunn - CPGA
Course Supt.: Ed Dunn
Architect: Arthur Murray

18 - R - 6514 - 73

Approximately 65 new sand traps, new clubhouse and outdoor swimming pool. A scenic course set upon rolling hills, it features three par 5's in a row.

| | |
|---|---|
| $$ | |
| Golf Pkgs. | Semi-Private |
| Power Carts | Lessons |
| Lounge | Snack Bar |
| Meals | |

## GOWAN BRAE GOLF & COUNTRY CLUB

**BATHURST, N.B. (On Youghall Dr., off Rte. 134)**
**Telephone: (506)546-2707**

Manager: Keith Dougherty
Head Pro: Eric St. George
Course Supt.: Gilbert Vienneau
Architect: C.E. "Robbie" Robinson

18 - R - 6553 - 72

This course has been reffered to as the "Pebble Beach of New Brunswick" by SCORE magazine. There is a view of the Bay on 14 of the 18 holes.

| | |
|---|---|
| $$ | |
| Golf Pkgs. | Semi-Private |
| Power Carts | Lessons |
| Lounge | Snack Bar |
| Meals | |

## HAMPTON COUNTRY CLUB

**HAMPTON, N.B. (On Smithtown Rd., off Rte. #1, toward the town of Hampton.)**
**Telephone: (506)832-3407**

President: Ivan Henry
Head Pro: Duncan Mayberry
Course Supt.: Darren Holt
Architect:Cecil Manuge

18 - R - 6193 - 72
This course has a 236 yard par 3 on #10, a 666 yard par 6 on #6, and a long carry over water on #5. The entire course is quite hilly.

| | |
|---|---|
| $$ | |
| Golf Pkgs. | Semi-Private |
| Power Carts | Lessons |
| Lounge | Snack Bar |
| | |

## HERRING COVE PROVINCIAL PARK GOLF COURSE

**CAMPOBELLO ISLAND, N.B. (Cross international bridge from Lubec Maine)**
**Park Office: (506)752-2369** **Pro Shop: (506)752-2449**
**Toll Free: 1-800-442-4442**

Owner: Province of New Brunswick
Head Pro: Bruce Vantassel - CPGA
Course Supt.: Clinton Calder - CGSA
Architect: Jeffrey Cornish

9 - R - 2901 - 36

Scenic views of the Bay of Fundy with a campground adjacent for accommodations. Historic Roosevelt Campobello International Park nearby. For more information see our full page ad on the facing page.

| | |
|---|---|
| $$ | |
| | Public |
| Power Carts | Lessons |
| Lounge | Snack Bar |
| Meals | |

## MACTAQUAC PROVINCIAL PARK GOLF CLUB

**MACTAQUAC, N.B. (On Rte #105, from Hwy. 2, at exit #274)**
**Telephone: (506)363-4139** **Fax: (506)363-3690**

Owner: Province of New Brunswick
Head Pro: Alan Howie
Course Supt.: Ken Creighton
Architect: William F. Mitchell

18 - R - 6423 - 72
Recognized as one of the great golf courses in Canada, it will be host to the Priority Courier Classic, an Atlantic C.P.G.A. event. Long, wide fairways with deer crossings on most holes. For more information see our ad on page 26.

| | |
|---|---|
| $$ | |
| Golf Pkgs. | Public |
| Power Carts | Lessons |
| Lounge | Snack Bar |
| Meals | |

## MAGNETIC HILL GOLF & COUNTRY CLUB

**MONCTON, N.B. (Off Hwy 2 at exits 488 A or B, at world famous Magnetic Hill)**
**Telephone: (506)858-1611** **Fax: (506)858-8901**

Manager: Kent Clarke
Head Pro: Jamie Van Wart
Course Supt.: Len Killam
Architect: Jimmy Johnstone

18 - R - 5670 - 69

This course is a mixture of flat and hilly terrain.
Located next to Magnetic Hill it offers picturesque views.

| | |
|---|---|
| $$ | |
| Golf Pkgs. | Semi-Private |
| Power Carts | Lessons |
| Lounge | Snack Bar |
| | |

## WESTFIELD GOLF & COUNTRY CLUB

**WESTFIELD, N.B. (Westfield exit off Rte. #7 to Rte #102, turn R. at intersection)**
**Telephone: (506)757-2250**

Manager: Tony Smith
Head Pro: Bobby Barr
Course Supt.: Paul Marr
Architects: Donald Ross/C.E. "Robbie" Robinson

18 - R - 5699 - 69
Located on a hill overlooking the Saint John River, the "Rhine of North America".

| | |
|---|---|
| $$ | |
| Golf Pkgs. | Semi-Private |
| Power Carts | Lessons |
| Lounge | Snack Bar |
| Meals | |

# GOLF *at*

**HERRING COVE GOLF COURSE,** ***Campobello Island, N.B.***

Scenic 9 hole course overlooking Bay of Fundy ■ Golf Professional and Pro Shop ■ Licenced Restaurant ■ Provincial Park and Campground ■ Beautiful salt water beach ■ Hiking Trails and Whale Watching Tours ■ Historic Roosevelt International Park

***Pro Shop (506) 752-2449   Campground (506) 752-2396***

***Off U.S. Route 1, 60 miles from St. Stephen, N.B.***

New Nouveau
**Brunswick**
***Provincial Parks***

# GOLF *at*

**MACTAQUAC PARK GOLF COURSE,** ***Mactaquac, N.B.***
Championship 18 hole course ■ One of Canada's premier courses ■ Featured in "The Great Courses of Canada" by J. Gordon ■ Host of 1992 Atlantic Classic ■ Golf Professional and Pro Shop ■ Licenced Restaurant and Lounge ■ Provincial Park and Campground ■ Marina and supervised swimming ■ Self-guided Hiking Trails

***Pro Shop (506) 363-4139   Park (506) 363-3011***
***Fax. (506) 363-3690***
***On Highway 105, 18 miles west of Fredericton, N.B.***

New Nouveau
**Brunswick**
***Provincial Parks***

Enjoy Unlimited Golfing
By-the-Sea...
12
1
11
10
9
8
At The Algonquin Resort, spend the whole day golfing with our fabulous 'Golf By The Sea' package for two! You'll feel the ocean breeze on our splendid 18-hole and 9-hole courses, both a leisurely 5-minute walk away. We'll even start you off with plenty of tees and three golf balls per person, plus complimentary continental breakfasts. Enjoy golfing the way it was meant to be...at The Algonquin!
$149.00 per night (single), plus taxes
$199.00 per night (double), plus taxes
Atlantic Canada's Golf
RESORT
Canadian Pacific Hotels & Resorts
The Algonquin
St. Andrews By-the-Sea, New Brunswick E0G 2X0
Managed by Canadian Pacific Hotels and Resorts for Algonquin Properties Limited, a company wholly-owned by the Province of New Brunswick.
For reservations and information, call (506)529-8823 or toll-free 1-800-268-9411 (Canada) or 1-800-828-7447 (U.S.A.)

Best Western
INDEPENDENT WORLDWIDE LODGING

# Claymore Inn
# Antigonish Conference Centre

## Special Foursome Deluxe Golf Package

Deluxe Apartment Suites
4 Beds
2 Bathrooms
Living Room
Dining Room
Kithcen
Adjacent to 24 hour supermarket
and Antigonish Mall

*other fantastic "budget-wise" Golf Packages available*

Antigonish has a reputation as a beautiful area for holiday fun and now with its newly expanded 18-hole golf course, it is quickly becoming a golfer's paradise. The Antigonish Golf & Country Club is a well designed, professionally developed course and has over 6600 yards of some of the most challenging golfing in Nova Scotia.
For more details on the course see page opposite.

ANTIGONISH GOLF & COUNTRY CLUB

TO BOOK YOUR GOLF GETAWAY CONTACT:

Best Western Claymore Inn / Antigonish Conference Centre

**(902)863-0123**

Reservations Toll Free:
**1-800-528-1234**

P.O. Box #1720, Church Street, Antigonish, N.S. B2G 2M5

## *Golfing in Nova Scotia*

*Nova Scotia is home to 45 beautiful golf courses, many of them unexcelled in beauty and challenge. Natural hazards are provided by the ocean as you head up lush green fairways that jut into the blue Atlantic. Your shot may be played against a back-ground of sails from an offshore schooner or framed by a stand of tall pines.*

*There are eight courses near the metropolitan area of Halifax and Dartmouth, Nova Scotia's largest urban area.*

*The Annapolis Valley region boasts a golf course every 20 miles. From Digby to Falmouth, there are six 18-hole courses and two 9-hole courses. This region of the province gets more sunshine than any other area of Atlantic Canada, and the fairways and greens are always in top condition.*

*Along the South Shore region of the province there are seven golf clubs and on the Glooscap Trail there are four.*

*Perhaps the best known is the Cape Breton Highlands Links, Ingonish Beach, on the rugged Cabot Trail. Designed in the early 1930s by well-known Canadian Architect Stanley Thompson, its scenery, wildlife and challenge make it one of the most popular courses in Atlantic Canada.*

*For More Information Contact: Nova Scotia Tourism & Culture*

*4th. Floor, Cornwallis Place,*
*1601 Water Street, Halifax, N.S. Canada B3J 3C6*
*Tel: (902) 424-5000*

## ANTIGONISH GOLF & COUNTRY CLUB

**ANTIGONISH, N.S. (Off Cloverville Rd., off College St., minutes from downtown)**
**Telephone: (902)863-4797**

Head Pro: Edwin Ryan
Course Supt.: Mike MacLellan
Architect: Robert Moote

18 - R - 6190 - 72

Home of the Annual *"Kilted Golf Tournament"*.
This course offers a scenic view of the entire town.
The 11th hole is a par-3 with the tee 120 feet above the green.

| | |
|---|---|
| $$ | |
| Golf Pkgs. | Public |
| Power Carts | Lessons |
| Lounge | Snack Bar |
| Meals | |

# Dundee
## RESORT

*Dundee is Dundee. A beautiful and friendly place - a holiday resort conveniently located between Port Hawksbury and Sydney on the Bras d'Or Lakes, Cape Breton Island.*

*Dundee Resort offers an 18-hole professionally designed golf course, 39 fully equipped housekeeping cottages set in the hillside, overlooking the lakes, a marina with 28 seasonal and 4 daily berths, tennis, swimming pool, children's playground, and boat rentals.*

*The licensed dining room offers an appetizing selection of fresh seafood and home style meals each evening as well as a daily luncheon menu. Relax before and after dinner in the lounge.*

**GOLF PACKAGES AVAILABLE**

from **$91.00** (per person / quad occ.)

Includes:

- 2 nights accommodation (two bedroom cottage)
- 3 days unlimited golf
- unlimited use of 1 golf cart
- unlimited use of resort facilities

FOR MORE INFORMATION AND RESERVATIONS CONTACT:

**Dundee Resort**

**(902)345-2649 Toll Free: 1-800-565-5660**

R.R. #2 West Bay, Cape Breton, N.S. Canada B0E 3K0

## DUNDEE RESORT

**WEST BAY, N.S. (Take Route #4 to Cape Breton Island and follow the signs)**

**Reservations: (902)345-2649** **Golf Course: (902)345-2639**

**Toll Free: 1-800-565-5660**

Manager: Graham Hudson
Head Pro: Bobby Hussey
Architect: Robert Moote

18 - R - 6100 - 72

This course is well known for its steep elevations and beautiful views of Bras d'Or Lake.

| | |
|---|---|
| $$ | Resort |
| Golf Pkgs. | Public |
| Power Carts | Lessons |
| Lounge | Snack Bar |
| Meals | |

HIGHLANDS LINKS

## HIGHLANDS LINKS

**INGONISH BEACH, N.S. (Drive the internationally famous Cabot Trail to Ingonish)**
**Pro Shop: (902)285-2600 Park Office: (902)285-2866**

Owner: Cape Breton Highlands National Park (Canada Parks)
Head Pro: Joe Robinson - CPGA
Course Supt.: Martin Walsh
Architect: Stanley Thompson

18 - R - 6198 - 71

Unforgiving rough, wee undulating Scottish greens and changeable swirling ocean weather offer stratigic challenges reminiscent of some of Scotland's historic courses. This course is designed to be played, enjoyed and experienced on foot.

| | |
|---|---|
| $ | Resort |
| Golf Pkgs. | Public |
| | Lessons |
| Lounge | Snack Bar |
| | |

NORTHUMBERLAND SEASHORE GOLF LINKS
N S G L
PUGWASH N.S.

## NORTHUMBERLAND SEASHORE GOLF LINKS

**PUGWASH, N.S. (On Gulf Shore Rd., in Pugwash, off Rte. #6 from Amherst)**
**Telephone: (902)243-2910**

Manager: R.A. (Ron) Mackenzie
Course Supt.: John W. Mills
Architects: Jeffrey Cornish/ C.E. "Robbie" Robinson

18 - R - 6192 - 72

This course features open and tree lined fairways with some "links" style holes right on the ocean. Fast and true greens present a real challenge.

| | |
|---|---|
| $$ | |
| | Public |
| Power Carts | |
| Lounge | Snack Bar |
| Meals | |

DRIVE CAREFULLY
Thank you for visiting . . .
ATLANTIC CANADA
. . . Come again soon

GOLF CONNECTIONS

# FLORIDA

Pages 33-64

Captiva Island Golf Course

1992/93 DIRECTORY

# *Golf Vacations*

## FLORIDA
Pages 33-64

GOLF CONNECTIONS

## BAYMEADOWS GOLF CLUB

**JACKSONVILLE, FL (On Baymeadows Rd., E. off I-95)**
**Telephone: (904)731-5705 Fax: (904)733-0236**

Manager: Norm Haglund
Head Pro: Roy Jarvis
Course Supt.: John Freeburn
Architects: Desmond Muirhead/Gene Sarazen

18 - R - 6250 - 72
Four sets of tees make this course extremely playable for all skill levels. It offers complete practice facilities and is "Home of the McCumber Golf School".

| | |
|---|---|
| $$ | |
| Golf Pkgs. | Semi-Private |
| Power Carts | Lessons |
| Lounge | Snack Bar |
| Meals | Open All Year |

## BIG CYPRESS GOLF & COUNTRY CLUB

**LAKELAND, FL. (I-4 to exit 18, Hwy. 98 N. for 7 Mi.)**
**Telephone: (813)859-6871**

Head Pro: Jeff O'Malley - PGA
Course Supt.: Tony Disano
Architect: Ron Garl

18 - R - 5595 - 72
Rating: Men's - 66.8, Slope - 114

| | |
|---|---|
| $$ | |
| | Public |
| Power Carts | Lessons |
| | Snack Bar |
| | Open All Year |

## BOBBY JONES GOLF COMPLEX

**SARASOTA, FL. (Exit 39, off I-75, W. on Fruitville to Beneva, R. to Circus Blvd.)**
**Telephone: (813)955-8097**

Manager: Ray Grady
Head Pro: Robbie Sharpless
Asst. Pro: Dale Dickison
Architects: Donald Ross / Ron Garl

45 Holes: American course - 18 - R - 6009 - 71
British course - 18 - R - 6468 - 72
Gillespie course - 9 - Ex. - 1687 - 30

| | |
|---|---|
| $ | |
| Golf Pkgs. | Public |
| Power Carts | Lessons |
| Lounge | Snack Bar |
| Meals | Open All Year |

BENT OAK GOLF CLUB

## BENT OAK GOLF CLUB

**TITUSVILLE, FL. (On London Town Rd. in N. Titusville)**
**Telephone: (407)269-4653**

Owned & Operated: Carson's Group, Inc.
Dir. of Golf: Bob Carson - PGA
Head Pro: Al Effler - PGA

18 - R - 6177 - 71

Rating: Men's - 68.4 Ladies'- 69.3

Beautifully kept course set amidst great bent oak trees and other native flora.

| | |
|---|---|
| $$ | |
| Golf Pkgs. | Public |
| Power Carts | Lessons |
| Lounge | Snack Bar |
| Meals | Open All Year |

BLOOMINGDALE
Golfers Club

## BLOOMINGDALE GOLFERS CLUB

**VALRICO, FL (On Natures Way Blvd. 15-20 minutes from downtown Tampa)**
**Telephone: (813)685-4105 Fax: (813)654-1227**

Dir. of Golf: John Reger - PGA
Teaching Director: Tom McCrary
Designer: Ron Garl

18 - R - 6799 - 72

Peppered with pot bunkers, this course meanders through natural forests, swamplands, and marsh preserves, with sand and water to greet you at every opportunity. Ranked 9th in the State of Florida in 1990.

| | |
|---|---|
| $$$ | |
| Golf Pkgs. | Public |
| Power Carts | Lessons |
| Lounge | Snack Bar |
| Meals | Open All Year |

## COLONY WEST COUNTRY CLUB

**TAMARAC, FL (From I-95 & FL Tpk., take Commercial Blvd.,W. to Pine Island Rd.)**
**Telephone: (305)726-8430**

Gen. Mgr.: Norm Rack
Head Pro: Craig Rack - PGA
Course Supt.: Dale Kuehner
Architects: VonHagge / Devlin
36 Holes: *18 - R - 7271 - 71
18 - Ex. - 4624 - 65

*Regarded by *Golf Digest* as one of the best public courses in Florida. Listed in U.S.G.A.'s top 20 most challenging courses.Water comes in to play on 12 holes.

| | |
|---|---|
| $$$ | |
| Golf Pkgs. | Public |
| Power Carts | Lessons |
| Lounge | Snack Bar |
| Meals | Open All Year |

## GRAND PALMS GOLF & COUNTRY CLUB

**PEMBROKE PINES, FL. (W. on Pines Blvd., 1/4 Mi. past I-75)**
**Pro Shop: (305)437-3334** **Hotel: (305)431-8800**
**(call collect for reservations only)**

Sales Manager: Natalie Chasin
Head Pro: Richard Buskey - PGA
Designer: Ward Northrup

East Lake Course: 18 - R - 6727 - 71

| | |
|---|---|
| $$ | Resort |
| Golf Pkgs. | Public |
| Power Carts | Lessons |
| Lounge | Snack Bar |
| Meals | Open All Year |

## GLEN LAKES COUNTRY CLUB

**GLEN LAKES, FL (W. of Hwy. 19, between Weeki Watchee & Homosassa Springs)**
**Telephone: (904)597-9000 Can. Sales Office: (416)499-3333 or 1-800-222-9003**

Developers: William Allan Real Estate Co, Ltd.
Director of Golf: Jim Cocchi - USGA
Architect: Ron Garl

18 - Championship - 6669 - 72

Fairways sculptured through magestic oaks and pine trees. Many are split-tiered. Large contoured greens. Spring-fed, crystal clear lakes. Rated one of Florida's Ten Best New Courses for 1989.

## GRENELEFE RESORT

**HAINES CITY, FL (On State Rd. 546, 45 minutes from Orlando Intl. Airport)**
**Telephone: (813)422-7511 Toll Free: 1-800-237-9549**

Managing Director: Joseph Hunter
Golf Professionals: Randy Cahall/Howie Barrow

3 x 18 holes: East Course - R - 6802 - 72
South Course - R - 6869 - 71
West Course - R - 7325 - 72

Site of the PGA TOUR Qualifying School Finals - 1984/1991
Cadillac Florida Open July 1992.

| | |
|---|---|
| $$$ | Resort |
| Golf Pkgs. | Public |
| Power Carts | Lessons |
| Lounge | Snack Bar |
| Meals | Open All Year |

KILLEARN

**Killearn Country Club & Inn**

## KILLEARN COUNTRY CLUB & INN

**TALLAHASSEE, FL (On Hwy. 319, 1 Mi. N. of I-10 exit #30)**
**Telephone: 1-800-476-4101**

Manager: Jim Story
Head Pro: Marc Brady
Architect: W. Amick

27 Holes

Host of the LPGA Centel Classic.
For more details on this facility please see ad on page 45 of this section.

| | |
|---|---|
| $$$ | Resort |
| Golf Pkgs. | Private |
| Power Carts | Lessons |
| Lounge | Snack Bar |
| Meals | Open All Year |

KISSIMMEE GC
FLORIDA

## KISSIMMEE GOLF CLUB

**KISSIMMEE, FL (On Hoagland Blvd., 2-1/2 Mi. S. of Hwy. 192)**
**Telephone: (407)847-2816 Fax: (407)847-6358**

Manager: Rick Sargent
Head Pro: Rick Sargent
Course Supt.: Allen Brissenden
Architect: William Bulmer/Gordon Lewis

18 - R - 5980 - 72
A fun course to play, this club boasts some of the finest greens in central Florida. Adjacent to the Kissimmee Airport, it is just 10 minutes from Disney World.

| | |
|---|---|
| $$$ | |
| | Public |
| Power Carts | Lessons |
| Lounge | Snack Bar |
| Meals | Open All Year |

## LAUREL OAK COUNTRY CLUB

**SARASOTA, FL (On Gary Player Blvd., off Bee Ridge Rd.)**
**Telephone: (813)378-3600** **Estate Sales Office: (813)378-4466 or (813)378-4477**

Developers: Radnor/Sarasota Corporation
Director of Golf: Ron Montressor - USPGA, CPGA
Course Supt.: Mack Baugh
Architect: Gary Player

18 - R - 6676 - 72

Lehigh RESORT

## LEHIGH RESORT

**LEHIGH, FL (On Route 884, 13 Mi. from Ft. Myers exit #22, East off I-75)**
**Telephone: (813)369-2121**

General Manager: Michael Smith
Head Pro: Dave Deetscreek - PGA
Course Supt.: Tom Rainey

2 x 18 holes - North Course: 18 - R - 6115 - 71
South Course: 18 - R - 6490 - 72

The North course features small greens and narrow fairways demanding accuracy rather than distance. The South course is longer and requires distance with less emphasis on accuracy, but does feature well placed bunkers.

| | |
|---|---|
| $$$ | Resort |
| Golf Pkgs. | Public |
| Power Carts | Lessons |
| Lounge | Snack Bar |
| Meals | Open All Year |

OakFord

## OAKFORD GOLF CLUB

**SARASOTA, FL. (On Palm View Rd., East of I-75, off Fruitville Rd.)**
**Telephone: (813)371-3680**

Manager: Sue Hentz
Head Pro: Marty Dickerson
Course Supts: Doug Powell/Larry Keech
Architect: Ron Garl
3 x 9 Holes: Myrtle Course: 9 - R - 3404 - 36
Live Oaks Course: 9 - R - 3349 - 36
Palms Course: 9 - R - 3334 - 36

Individual lessons, group lessons and golf schools available.

| | |
|---|---|
| $$ | |
| Golf Pkgs. | Public |
| Power Carts | Lessons |
| Lounge | Snack Bar |
| Meals | Open All Year |

# Mission inn

GOLF AND TENNIS RESORT

Howey in-the Hills (Orlando) Florida

## A WORLD CLASS DESTINATION

TIMELESS YET EVER-CHANGING. . . this family owned and operated Mobil Four Star resort is a unique blend of casual elegance, superb service and world-class recreation. Mission Inn gracefully weaves excellence into every aspect of your stay. For a special treat, pamper yourself with a cruise aboard our exquisitely restored 1930's river yacht, La Reina.

## A GOLFER'S PARADISE

Mission Inn is a secluded oasis that welcomes guests with the grace and hospitality of a plush, private estate. Centre stage is its golf course with championship character that is evident with every great golf hole. Towering forests rise in quiet splendour to shade emerald fairways, and quiet lakes are witness to nature's wildlife. Always inviting. Always a challenge. And memorable no matter what the score.

## AMONG THE VERY BEST

Boasting rare 85' elevations tee to green and water on 13 holes, it's no wonder why Mission Inn is ranked 16th of Florida's 1,100 golf courses. January 1992 marked the opening of a second 18 hole course, a dynamic design by PGA Tour Player, Gary Koch.

10400 County Road 48, Howey-in-the-Hills, FL 34737
(904) 324-3101 Fax: (904) 324-3101 ext. 7443

RESERVATIONS
(800) 874-9053

GROUP SALES
(800) 523-2289

# PERDIDO BAY GOLF RESORT

**PENSACOLA, FL (On Doug Ford Drive)**
**Telephone: 1-800-874-5355 Fax: (904)492-1204**

Manager: Phil Wiggins
Director of Golf: Bud Cooper
Architect: W. Amick

18 - R - 7154 - 72

Host of the PGA Pensacola Open from 1978 to 1987. An unforgettable pearl on the Emerald Coast. See page opposite for more data.

| | |
|---|---|
| $$$ | Resort |
| Golf Pkgs. | Semi-Private |
| Power Carts | Lessons |
| Lounge | Snack Bar |
| Meals | Open All Year |

# PERDIDO BAY

GOLF DIGEST calls it *"One of the top 50 public courses in the country."* You'll call it a favorite. The 7154 yard Perdido Bay Tournament course has tested the skills of Sam Snead, Doug Ford, Arnold Palmer, Gay Brewer, and a host of other winners. An unforgetable pearl on the emerald coast. Home of the PGA Pensacola Open (1978-87). The course record of 62 was set by Curtis Strange during the Pensacola Open.

Golf Villas located right on the course offer packages starting at $49.50 per person.

FOR RESERVATIONS CALL:
1-800-874-5355 (US & Canada)

One Doug Ford Drive Pensacola, FL 32507

---

KILLEARN

# Killearn Country Club & Inn

Experience the serene southern beauty of Killearn Country Club and Inn nestled in the rolling hills just a few miles north of Florida's capital city. Home of the prestigious LPGA ***CENTEL*** **CLASSIC**, Killearn offers a complete range of amenities including their top rated challenging 27-hole golf course, swimming pool, tennis courts, deluxe hotel accommodations and superb dining.

Inn and Lodge facilities located right on the course offer packages starting at $49.50 per person

FOR RESERVATIONS CALL:
1-800-476-4101 (US & Canada)

100 Tyron Circle • Tallahassee, Florida 32308

# EVERYTHING... BUT THE CROWDS.

The Plantation Inn and Golf Resort is not your typical Florida resort. Quiet. Gracious. Unassuming. And the only thing missing are the crowds.

**The Golf School.** You'll learn more in a five day vacation than most golfers learn in a lifetime. The Golf School boasts one of the most impressive reputations of any golf school in the country. Established in 1978, it's graduated more than 32,000 golfers.

The Golf School's unique, flexible program makes it the popular choice for players of all abilities. Whether you're an absolute beginner, the casual weekend player or an aspiring pro, The Golf School is for you. Just check your score card at the end of your stay.

**Great Golf Getaways.** The Plantation's flexible golf getaway packages allow you to play 27 outstanding holes on one of our courses or choose among six other courses carefully selected for the greatest variety in golfing vacations. And all of our golf packages include outstanding accommodations and breakfast each morning.

**For Reservations And Information Call 800-632-6262**

Plantation Inn and Golf Resort

CRYSTAL RIVER

## RAVINES COUNTRY CLUB

**MIDDLEBURG, FL (13 Mi. S. of Jacksonville on S/R 21(Blanding Blvd) L. on C/R 218 then left 7/10 Mi.)**
**Telephone: (904)282-7888** **Inn: (904)282-1111**

Manager: Steve Monahan
Head Pro: Tim Hooks
Course Supt.: Keith Smith
Architect: McCumber Golf

18 - R - 6784 - 72
One of the most spectacular, natural golf course settings.

| | |
|---|---|
| $$ | Resort |
| Golf Pkgs. | Public |
| Power Carts | Lessons |
| Lounge | Snack Bar |
| Meals | Open All Year |

## THE RIVER CLUB

**BRADENTON, FL (1-1/2 Mi. E. of I-75 off exit 41)**
**Telephone: (813)751-4211**

Gen. Mgr: Mike Pascuzzi
Head Pro: Tommy Smith - PGA
Course Supt.: George Cook
Architect: Ron Garl

18 - R - 6600 - 72
Undulating fairways and greens. Nominated as one of the top new golf courses in the country by Golf Digest.

| | |
|---|---|
| $$ | |
| Golf Pkgs. | Public |
| Power Carts | Lessons |
| Lounge | Snack Bar |
| Meals | Open All Year |

..."THEY'RE WAITING AT THE MAGIC KINGDOM, LETS DO NINE HOLES QUICK!"

## ROYAL OAK GOLF CLUB

**TITUSVILLE, FL (On Country Club Dr. I-95 to Hwy.50, to St. Rd. 405, to Park Ave.)**
**Telephone: (407) 269-4500**

Owners: Canadian PGA
Gen. Mgr./Dir. of Golf: Steven W. Hill
Course Supt.: Bob Snapp
Architects: Robert Von Hagge / Dick Wilson

18 - R - 6709 - 71
Well maintained, rolling course with eight crystal clear lakes. A genuine challenge for the discriminating golfer.

| | |
|---|---|
| $$ | |
| | Public |
| Power Carts | Lessons |
| Lounge | Snack Bar |
| Meals | Open All Year |

# TIMBERWOODS

## . . . a friendly, affordable vacation village

It's a world-class, family oriented resort village with a neighbourhood ambiance, and it offers a suprisingly affordable vacation choice all year round in Sarasota.

That in a few words, is what you will find at Tmberwoods, a unique little vacation world all of its own.

Located just south of Sarasota proper at 7964 Timberwood Circle (just off Beneva Road) near Sarasota Square Mall, Timberwoods is a vacation community of 112 villas - all sandy-hued with red tile roofs and arranged in several circular groupings.

The village is nestled in a lovely park-like setting, complete with its own lake. Here pines and palm trees grow in profusion, along with hibiscus, laurel shrubs, bouganvillea and other subtropical plantings.

Each air conditioned, tastefully furnished villa contains 1400 sq. ft. divided into two bedrooms, two baths, a living room, a dining room, a kitchen, and a screened verandah - plenty of room for four to six people. All units have fully equipped kitchens, a garage with automatic controls and a washer and dryer.

Amenities at Timberwoods include a large swimming pool and spa, two tennis courts, bicycles for young and old, miniature golf, shuffleboard courts, horseshoe pits, a putting green, a children's playground, pingpong tables, a barbeque area and a clubhouse with more indoor games and a well stocked library.

Opened in 1986, Timberwoods was built in a rural setting that remains close to Sarasota beaches and other attractions.

Challenging golf courses (open to public play) are within a short drive of Timberwoods and are plentiful. Golfers have no problem securing starting times even if they wished to play a different course each day.

Guests of Timberwoods are literally only two or three minutes away from a 24 hour food market, 12 movie theaters and three shopping centers, including the huge Sarasota Square Mall.

For more information call toll free at 1-800-824-5444. The local telephone number is (813)923-4966. Fax (813)924-3109

. . . . . . . . . . . . . . . .

## TIMACUAN GOLF & COUNTRY CLUB

**LAKE MARY, FL (On Timacuan Blvd., off Rinehart Rd, from I-4, exit 50, Lk. Mary)**
**Telephone: (407)645-4653 Fax: (407)323-6671**

President: Patricia Stenstrom
Head Pro: David Moore
Course Supt.: Mark Stenstrom
Architect: Ron Garl

18 - R - 6582 - 72

Ranked #14 in Florida by *GOLFWEEK* and *FLORIDA GOLFER* magazine.

| | |
|---|---|
| $$$ | |
| Golf Pkgs. | Public |
| Power Carts | Lessons |
| Lounge | Snack Bar |
| Meals | Open All Year |

## UNIVERSITY PARK COUNTRY CLUB

**UNIVERSITY PARK, FL ( On University Parkway 1.8 Mi. W. of I-75, exit 40)**
**Telephone: (813)359-9999 Fax: (813)351-7778**

General Manager: Dale Weidemiller
Master Professional: Mike Clayton - PGA
Course Supt.: John Hagan
Architect Ron Garl

| | |
|---|---|
| $$ | |
| | Public |
| Power Carts | Lessons |
| Lounge | Snack Bar |
| Meals | Open All Year |

18 - R - 6500 - 72
One of the most beautiful and meticulously maintained golf courses in Florida. Thousands of flowers, bushes, shrubs and trees blend harmoniously with nature making each hole increasingly inviting and enjoyable. Five sets of tees.

THE
VENICE
GOLF AND COUNTRY CLUB

## VENICE GOLF & COUNTRY CLUB

**VENICE, FL. (Bypass 41, 3 Mi. E. on Centre Rd., entrance on N. side)**
**Telephone: (813)493-3400**

Dir. of Sales/Mktg.: Ed Edsell
Course Supt.: Troy Smith
Architect: Ted McAnlis

18 - R - 6710 - 72
Designed by The Evans Group, award-winning community planners, The Venice Golf & Country Club offers the best of golf and the finest of amanities.It is situated on 460 picturesque acres of lush woodlands and verdent grasslands.

DAYTONA BEACH GOLF GETAWAYS

A Daytona Beach Golf Getaway is more than just a great vacation. It's a great vacation value! With over 26 challenging golf courses in the Daytona Beach area, you can golf all year-round under the warm Florida Sunshine.

But that's not all!! Daytona is home to one sandtrap you won't want to avoid: one of the prettiest, sandiest, most magnificent beaches in the world.

We're also home to the LPGA and Daytona International Speedway. Kennedy Space Centre is just a chip shot away.

Plus, we'reonly an hour's drive from the magic of Walt Disney World*, EPCOT* and all of Central Florida's world famous attractions.

From sea to tee, it's sun and fun for the entire family - at prices so low you'll be able to stay an extra day or two!

For immediate information and reservations call any of the Hotel toll free numbers listed on the opposite page. For other information . . . call Daytona Beach Golf Getaways.

**1-800-854-1234**

Post Office Box 910
Daytona Beach, Florida 32115

**DAYTONA BEACH GOLF GETAWAYS**

Daytona Beach Resort Area • Palm Coast

# DAYTONA BEACH GOLF GETAWAYS

**Call Direct For More Information**

## *ACCOMMODATIONS:*

| | |
|---|---|
| Acapulco Inn | 800-874-7420 |
| Beachcomer Inn Beach Resort | 800-874-7420 |
| Best Western La Playa Resort | 800-874-6996 |
| Casa Del Mar | 800-874-7420 |
| Comfort Inn Oceanfront | 800-325-0099 |
| Coral Sands Inn/Seaside Cottages | 904-441-1831 |
| Days Inn Oceanfront South | 800-874-6996 |
| Daytona Beach Hilton | 800-525-7350 |
| Dayton Beach Marriott Resort | 800-872-9269 |
| Daytona Inn Broadway | 800-874-1822 |
| El Caribe Resort & Conf. Centre | 800-445-9889 |
| Granada Inn | 800-874-6996 |
| Holiday Inn Speedway | 800-227-7528 |
| Howard Johnson Hotel & Conf. Centre | 800-767-4471 |
| Howard Johnson Oceanfront | 800-874-6996 |
| Indigo Lakes Hilton Golf & Tennis Resort | 904-258-6333 |
| Mailsail Motel | 800-843-5142 |
| Newport beach Motel | 800-847-8811 |
| Palm Plaza Oceanfront Motel | 800-448-2286 |
| Perry's Ocean Edge Resort | 800-447-0002 |
| Pirates Cove Hotel | 800-233-2683 |
| Quality Inn Oceanside | 800-227-7220 |
| Quality Inn on the Oceanfront | 800-874-0975 |
| Ramada Inn Surfside | 800-255-3838 |
| Rodeway Inn Oceanfront | 800-262-7327 |
| Sheraton Palm Coast Resort | 904-445-3000 |
| SeaGarden Inn | 800-874-7420 |
| Sun Viking Lodge | 800-874-4469 |
| Treasure Island Inn | 800-874-7420 |

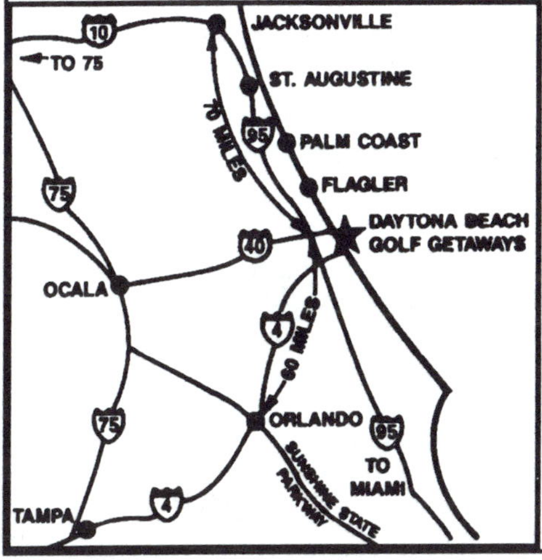


## *GOLF COURSES PARTICIPATING:*

- Cypress Head
- Cypress Knoll Golf Club
- Halifax Plantation
- Indigo Lakes
- Matanzas Woods
- Palm Harbor
- Pelican Bay South
- Pine Lakes Country Club
- River Bend Golf Club

*See details on courses as listed alphabetically in this section.*

# DAYTONA BEACH HILTON

*The Best on the Beach*

2637 South Atlantic Avenue • Daytona Beach, Florida 32118

Enjoy Florida's exciting new golf destination with value-priced golf packages at the Dayton Beach Hilton. We're everything you expect from Hilton plus miles of white sand, blue surf, and all the area's challenging courses nearby. There has never been a better time to come hit the links or surf with us.

## GOLF PACKAGES

| | | |
|---|---|---|
| Rate, Daily | from | $60.00 |
| Non-Golfer | from | $32.00 |
| 3 Night/4 Day | from | $164.00 |
| 6 Night/7 Day | from | $323.00 |

Rates are per person, double occupancy and are subject to availability.

**VALUE-PRICED GOLF PACKAGES INCLUDE:**

• Large, Luxurious Room with Refrigerator
• One Round of Golf per Night's Stay
• Welcome Cocktail • Welcome Gift
• American Breakfast Daily
• Free Daily Newspaper
• All Room and Sales Taxes

Daytona Beach Hilton guests also enjoy free valet parking, private direct beach access, uncrowded beach, oceanfront pool, whirlpool spa, lighted tennis courts, fitness roon with sauna, two lounges, two restaurants with casual and fine dining, (Roof Restaurant with spectacular ocean view voted the areas best) Accommodations include free HBO with remote control TVs, wet bars, refrigerators, hairdryers, and children may stay for free in parents' room.

*Located directly on the ocean on Highway A1A. I-95 Exit 85, east to A1A, then north 2 miles*

FOR MORE INFORMATION AND RESERVATIONS:

**CALL 1-800-525-7350 or 904-767-7350**
**FAX 904-760-3651**

DAYTONA BEACH GOLF GETAWAYS

# DAYTONA INN

**- OCEANFRONT -**
**HEART OF DAYTONA BEACH**

DAYTONA INN / BROADWAY is ideally located on the corner of Broadway (US92) and South Atlantic Avenue (A1A) on the beach.

The Inn is a family owned and operated, AAA Three Diamond Rated motel offering you that personal attention to make your golf holiday carefree and special.

## PERSONALIZED GOLF HOLIDAY PACKAGES

For a brochure and a no obligation price quote for a golf package *designed for your needs. . .*

Tel: 1-800-874-1822 (Canada & US) or Fax: (904) 255-3680.

Your Personal Golf Package can include:

- Breakfast
- Dine-a-round dinners
- Golf as many days as you want
- Oceanfront or non-oceanfront view
- Rooms or one bedroom suites
- King size or extra long double beds
- Rental car
- Groups, couples or individuals
- Day, week or month stays

Health club, Checkers Cafe, and heated, outdoor, oceanfront swimming pool are some of the amenities in all golf packages.

NO OBLIGATION - Call for your own Golf Holiday Package !!!

**DAYTONA INN / BROADWAY**

219 South Atlantic Ave., Daytona Beach, FL 32118
Tel: (904) 252-3626

# HOWARD JOHNSON®

Hotel & Conference Center
*Beachfront*

600 North Atlantic Avenue • Daytona Beach, FL 32118
(904) 255-4471

*Convenience and luxury you can afford . . . and right in the heart of Daytona Beach . . . that's what Howard Johnson Hotel is all about. We are oceanfront adjacent to Seabreeze Boulevard hosting great restaurants, nightlife and shopping. We are only minutes away from the Daytona Beach Airport, Daytona International Speedway, Jai Alai and Daytona Beach Kennel Club. With our location you are just a short distance from the area's greatest golf courses. Our newly remodeled "Legends" Restaurant and Lounge features racing memorabilia.*

## GOLF PACKAGES

| | | |
|---|---|---|
| No Frills Daily* | from | **$39.00** |
| Daily Package | from | **$58.00** |
| 3 nights / 4 days | from | **$168.00** |
| 5 nights / 6 days | from | **$280.00** |
| 7 nights / 8 days | from | **$392.00** |

Rates are per person, double occupancy
* No Frills package includes: Room and Golf ONLY

## PACKAGE FEATURES

- *Oceanview accommodations*
- *Complimentary welcome drink*
- *Complimentary continental breakfast daily*
- *Complimentary dinner each evening, or dine-around vouchers*
- *18 holes of golf per day*
- *Tennis, volleyball, basketball on pool deck*
- *Group rates available • Single golfer rates available*
- *Golf widow packages available*

FOR MORE INFORMATION AND RESERVATIONS CALL:

**TOLL FREE 1-800-767-4471**

DAYTONA BEACH GOLF GETAWAYS

## INDIGO LAKES HILTON

**DAYTONA BEACH, FL. (On Volusia Ave.)**
**Telephone: (904)258-6333** **Florida Toll Free: 1-800-223-4161**

Manager: Lon Yaeger
Head Pro: Tom Ferguson
Course Supt.: Dave Van Wagner
Architect: Lloyd Clifton

18 - R - 6176 - 72
Extensive renovations have just been completed on this award winning golf course. Indigo Lakes is one of the finest courses in the Daytona Beach area.

| | |
|---|---|
| $$ | Resort |
| Golf Pkgs. | |
| Power Carts | Lessons |
| Lounge | Snack Bar |
| Meals | Open All Year |

Quality Inn

**On The Beach**

1615 S. Atlantic Avenue
Daytona Beach, FL 32118
(904) 255-0921
**(800) 874-0975**

We know how you like to relax after a challenging round of golf because our management staff has been involved in some of America and Europe's best golf clubs. From our remarkably comfortable oceanfront rooms and suites, our airy lobby restaurant, to our intimate poolside lounge, you'll find the relaxed comradery of fellow golfers and sportsmen. Select the golf vacation package of your choice from our specially prepared offers, and we'll take care of providing the amenities you deserve for a great golf getaway in Daytona Beach!

| 1992 GOLF PACKAGES | | |
|---|---|---|
| **DAILY PACKAGE**<br>1 night/1 days play | from | $48 |
| **4 DAY STAY**<br>3 nights/3 days play | from | $133 |
| **6 DAY STAY**<br>5 nights/5 days play | from | $217 |

*All rates are per person, Double Occupancy. Based on space availablility, some black out dates apply. Packages include oceanfront rooms, green fees and taxes only. Other packages available.*

"We look forward to providing a quality golf vacation experience and the service you would expect from the staff of your home club"

*The Quality Inn on the Beach Staff*

FOR MORE INFORMATION AND RESERVATIONS:

**CALL (800) 874-0975 or (904) 255-0921**

DAYTONA BEACH GOLF GETAWAYS

# PLAY 72 HOLES OF CHAMPIONSHIP GOLF IN PALM COAST

Matanzas Woods
at Palm Coast

## MATANZAS WOODS GOLF CLUB

(904) 446-6330 Pro: Ed Crowell

*Arnold Palmer/Ed Seay Design*
*Par 72, 6985 yds., Slope 132, Rating 73.3*

Each hole of Matanzas Woods seems progressively tougher until the 13th tee – where our version of the "Amen Corner" begins. The 18th is a par 5 with a spectacular island green.

## PINE LAKES COUNTRY CLUB

(904) 445-0852 Pro: Ken VanLeuven

*Arnold Palmer/Ed Seay Design*
*Par 72, 7074 yds., Slope 126, Rating 73.5*

Sixty-three white sand bunkers, water on eleven holes and 7000+ yds. of length make Pine Lakes one of north-central Florida's most challenging courses.

pine lakes
COUNTRY CLUB
at Palm Coast

Cypress Knoll
at Palm Coast

## CYPRESS KNOLL GOLF CLUB

(904) 437-5807 Pro: Joe Gutterman

*Gary Player Signature Design*
*Par 72, 6591 yds., Slope 130, Rating 71.6*

Cypress Knoll rewards greens hit in regulation with realistic birdie opportunities, but don't be fooled by small, flat greens with gentle approaches – the rolling fairways are narrow and lined with hazards.

## PALM HARBOR GOLF CLUB

(904) 445-0845 Pro: Bud Burkley

*Bill Amick Design*
*Par 72, 6615 yds., Slope 127, Rating 71.8*

Palm Harbor's narrow, bending fairways lined with towering palms, oaks and pines combined with small elevated greens to demand accurate shot making.

Palm Harbor Golf Club
*at Palm Coast*

***Golf packages available through the Award Winning Sheraton Palm Coast Resort Call (800) 325-3535***

DRIVE CAREFULLY
Thank you for visiting . . .
FLORIDA
. . . Come again soon

GOLF CONNECTIONS

# GEORGIA

Pages 65-72

Jekyll Island, Georgia

1992/93 DIRECTORY

# Golf Vacations

## GEORGIA

Pages 65-72

GOLF CONNECTIONS

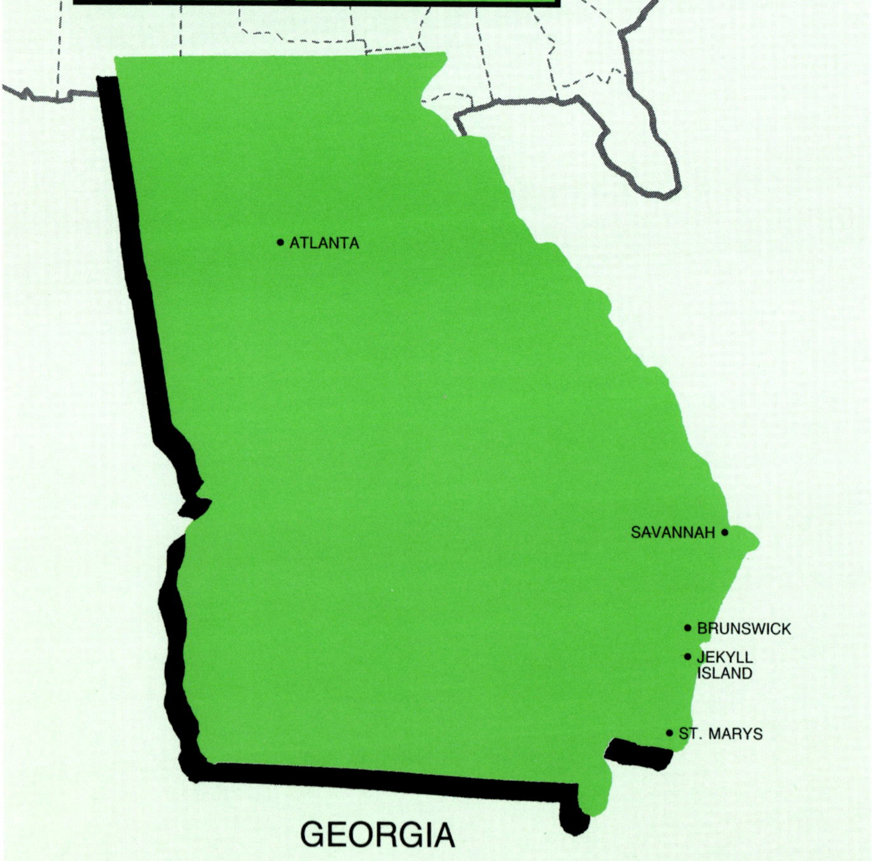


GEORGIA

# 189 Holes of Golf!

Come experience superb golf, year-round, in Brunswick & The Golden Isles. Tee it up and test your skills along miles of coastal Georgia's finest fairways at courses counted among the state's and nation's finest.

Plus, acres of tennis courts, miles of sun-drenched beaches, an ocean of sport fishing. Accommodations of every description and hospitality to match our sunny, inviting Fall climate.

Brunswick, Jekyll Island, St. Simons Island, Sea Island and Little St. Simons Island. All waiting just minutes from I-95. Send for your free vacation planning guide today, or call 1-800-933-COAST.

**Brunswick & The Golden Isles OF GEORGIA**

Jekyll Island • Little St. Simons Island
St. Simons Island • Sea Island

Name____________________

Address____________________

City__________ State______ Zip______

Mail to: Brunswick/Golden Isles Visitors Bureau
4 Glynn Avenue, Brunswick, GA 31520

GC

GEORGIA'S COLONIAL COAST

## OSPREY COVE GOLF COURSE

**ST. MARYS, GA (On St. Mary's Rd. 2 Mi. E. from GA Exit 1, off I-95)**
**Telephone: (912)882-5575 US Toll Free: 1-800-352-5575**

Head Pro: Darryl Jack
Course Supt.: Burr Johnson
Architect: Mark McCumber

18 - R - 6269 - 72

This course appeals to players of all levels. It provides an enjoyable golfing experience for the average player, yet can test even the best from the back tees.

| | |
|---|---|
| $$ | |
| Golf Pkgs. | Public |
| Power Carts | Lessons |
| Lounge | Snack Bar |
| Meals | Open All Year |

From November 15/91 to January 31st/92 Jekyll Island, long known for its picturesque beaches, championship golf and tennis and intriguing history, became a "Golfer's Heaven".

During that period, a special promotion offer was made to golfers *registering under a golf package* at any of the ten resort hotels or the rental cottages on Jekyll . . . NO GREEN FEES during his/her entire stay, no matter how long the stay or how many times they wished to play golf. All that had to be paid was cart rental.

Golfers who had never played Jekyll Island's courses and many who had let a number of years pass since last visiting this barrier island off the Georgia Coast were indeed pleasantly surprised.

Not only did they enjoy the NO GREEN FEE play, they were able to test their skills on courses that had seen more than $1.12 million in renovations and refinements.

Jekyll Island is Georgia's largest public golf resort with 63 holes of challenging golf. The main clubhouse on Capt. Wylly Road services three 18 hole courses . . . Oleander and Pine Lakes, both designed by legendary architect Dick Wilson, and Indian Mound created by Joe Lee.

The Oceanside 9 with a separate clubhouse on Shell Road, was laid out in 1898 for the exclusive Jekyll Island Club. No longer exclusive, it has played the same since its redesign in the 1920s by Walter J. Travis.

From December 1/92 to February 15/93 Jekyll Island will once again become "Golfer's Heaven". FREE GOLF. . . 18 holes/day. Cart rental required. This year the FREE GOLF is being limited to 18 holes/day to allow more folks to participate.

If you wish more information about golfing on Jekyll Island it can be obtained by writing the Jekyll Island Convention and Visitors Bureau, P.O. Box 3186, Jekyll Island, GA 31527 or you can call them at 1-800-841-6586 or (912) 635-3636.

## JEKYLL ISLAND - A "GOLFER'S HEAVEN"

### OLEANDER GOLF COURSE

*This beautiful 18-hole course designed by Dick Wilson cuts through woodlands and marshland giving you frequent glimpses of the Island's wildlife as you make your way around 6,679 yards - par 72. Fairways dogleg left and right while ocean winds often provide an additional challenge. With water coming into play on eight holes, this course rewards finesse and accuracy. Course rating is 72.0 and slope rating is 128.*

### PINE LAKES GOLF COURSE

*Bunkers guard almost every green on this rolling 6,802 yards - par 72 making Pine Lakes the longest and tightest course on the Island. Mounded fairways turn both left and right; and while this course is also a Dick Wilson design, it plays differently from Oleander, placing a real premium on an excellent short game. It is rated at 71.9 with a slope rating of 130.*

### INDIAN MOUND GOLF COURSE

*Joe Lee, whose credits include the Blue Monster at Doral, designed Jekyll's newest golf course to be as beautiful as it is challenging. While Oleander is famous for its water hazards and Pine Lakes for its bunkers, Indian Mound has it all. A 6,596 yard - par 72, the course features wide fairways with numerous fairway bunkers and big undulating greens. Carved through pine trees and marshes, this picturesque course has eight holes where water comes into play. Course rating is 71.1 and slope rating is 127.*

### OCEANSIDE 9

*In 1898 Rockefeller, Morgan, Pulitzer and other members of the exclusive Jekyll Island Club built the Island's first golf course. That very course, now with almost a hundred years of golfing tradition, forms the basis of Oceanside 9. Remodelled in the 1920's by architect Walter J. Travis, Oceanside is still an authentic links course built over the natural lay of the land. This 9-hole, 3,298 yard - par 36 features several elevated tees, huge greenside bunkers and small sloping greens. Prevailing winds from the adjacent Atlantic Ocean create an additional challenge. Course rating is 70.9, slope rating is 126.*

# Sheraton Savannah
## RESORT & COUNTRY CLUB

OUR GOLF PACKAGES WILL
SAVE YOU A BUNDLE

INCLUDES:

- Deluxe accommodations
- Unlimited green fees on one of Georgia's top ten courses, originally designed by Donald Ross
- Club Storage
- 2 Breakfasts & 2 Dinners (Gratuities included) Cart, Taxes extra

**MARCH 1, 1992 - NOVEMBER 8, 1992**

| 3 DAY / 2 NIGHT PACKAGE | ADDITIONAL NIGHTS: |
|---|---|
| **$182.60** p.p. / dbl. occ. | **$91.30** p.p / dbl. occ. |
| **$275.60** p.p. / single occ. | **$137.80** p.p. / single occ. |

**NOVEMBER 8, 1992 - DECEMBER 31, 1992**

| 3 DAY / 2 NIGHT PACKAGE | ADDITIONAL NIGHTS: |
|---|---|
| **$154.60** p.p. / dbl. occ. | **$77.30** p.p. / dbl. occ. |
| **$199.60** p.p / single occ. | **$99.80** p.p / single occ. |

Note: Prices are subject to change

FOR RESERVATIONS, CALL

**1-800-533-6706**

612 WILMINGTON ISLAND ROAD, SAVANNAH, GEORGIA 31410
Telephone: (912) 897-1612 • Fax: (912) 897-1612 ext. 7245

The Atlanta Convention & Visitors Bureau provides an annual publication devoted to help Atlanta Conventioneers and visitors take advantage of golfing opportunities throughout Georgia. Public and private courses that accept visitors are listed therein.

ATLANTA CONVENTION AND VISITORS BUREAU

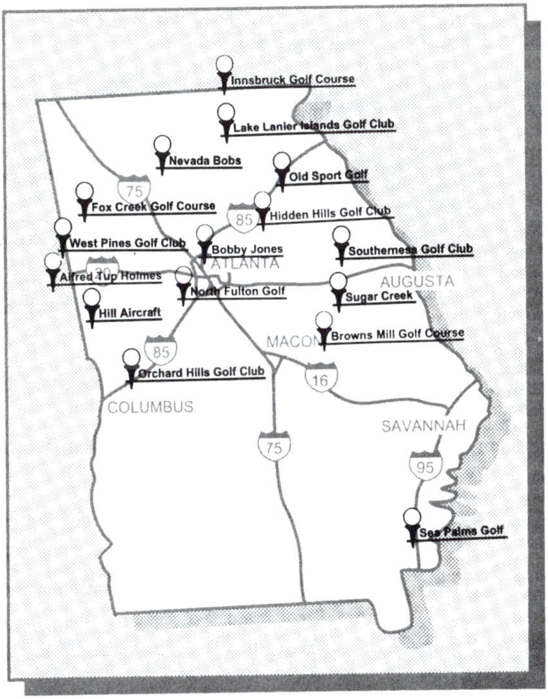


For more information contact:

**ATLANTA CONVENTION & VISITORS BUREAU**

**(404)521-6600**

233 Peachtree Street, Suite #2000, Atlanta, Georgia 30303

DRIVE CAREFULLY
Thank you for visiting . . .
GEORGIA
. . . Come again soon

# GOLF CONNECTIONS

# MICHIGAN

Heather G.C., Boyne

BEAUTIES and the BEASTS
17 magnificent 18 hole championship golf courses!
It's not a fairytale... it's Gaylord!
GAYLORD
MICHIGAN
Golf Mecca of the Midwest
Call today for your FREE full color Golf Travel Planner.
1 800 345-8621

DISCOVER GOLF
ON MICHIGAN'S Sunrise Side
FREE
"SUNRISE SIDE
GOLF TRAVEL PLANNER"
1-800-729-9373
GOLF
CART &
LODGING
from
$36 PER DAY
ELK RIDGE
GOLF COURSE

1992/93 DIRECTORY

# Golf Vacations

## MICHIGAN

Pages 73-88

GOLF CONNECTIONS

## The Super Five Golf Courses

## BOYNE MOUNTAIN.

THE MONUMENT:
*A scenic mile long golf cart ride takes you to the summit of this 7086 yard jewel. Four sets of tees drop in giant steps to the pond-protected first hole. You end up at the 18th. island hole that Sam Snead calls one of the most intimidating anywhere.The Monument was a GOLF DIGEST runner-up for Best New Resort Course of 1987.*

THE ALPINE:
*The Alpine also starts at the Mountain's summit, dropping down in swoops to Deer Lake. Spectacular views are everywhere. Fairways are wide and inviting. Blind shots are non-existent. For all of its innocence, strategic bunkers and water hazards can take their toll. Like all Boyne courses, optional tees on holes make it enjoyable whatever one's playing ability. Woods and spaces separate players. During a round you will probably encounter more furry and feathered friends than golfers.*

## BOYNE HIGHLANDS.

THE MOOR:
*Don't forget your sana wedge and ball retriever when you take on this Highland's test. You may need more than your driver. Besides the sand and water, there are marshes, woods, doglegs, and slick, tough-to-read greens. You should tackle The Moor with plenty of golf balls and good humor. The low handicappers who know all five Boyne courses consider it the most difficult. However it is much more forgiving when played from the forward tees.*

THE HEATHER:
*In 1971 the Highland's Heather course, designed by Robert Trent Jones, was recognized by GOLF DIGEST as one of America's 100 greatest courses. In 1979 GOLF DIGEST ranked it* ***the best*** *of all Michigan public, semi-private and resort courses. Heavily wooded with greens of 7,000 to 10,000 square feet, the layout is typical Jones. Water comes into play on 8 of the first 9 holes. Deep bunkers front or encircle greens. You'll like the challenge and love the course.*

THE DONALD ROSS MEMORIAL:
*Donald Ross is recognized as the father of golf course architecture in America, and he designed many of the country's classic courses. It's said, "You don't change a Donald Ross course, you copy it." Boyne went beyond mere copying, by duplicating 18 of his finest holes from such famous courses as Pinehurst No. 2, Oakland Hills, Seminole, Inverness and Royal Dornach. The course is strategic rather than penal. As Ross would say, playing it is "a pleasure, not a pennance."*

**FOR MORE INFORMATION CALL:1-800-GO-BOYNE**

## ANTRIM DELLS GOLF CLUB

**ELLSWORTH, MI (On Rte. #31, 12 Mi. S. of Charlevoix, 30 Mi. N. of Traverse City)**
**Telephone: (616)599-2679** **US Toll Free: 1-800-872-8561**
**Fax: (616)599-2113**

Architect: Jerry Mathews

18 - R - 6670 - 72

| | |
|---|---|
| $$ | |
| | Public |
| Power Carts | |
| Lounge | Snack Bar |
| Meals | |

Beautifuly wooded course overlooking Grand Traverse Bay.
Former Co-Host of the Michigan Amateur. Call for more information.

## CATTAILS GOLF CLUB

**SOUTH LYON, MI (On West 9 Mile Road)**
**Telephone: (313)486-8777**

Dir. of Golf: Robert B. Williams
Golf Pros: David Sias Jr./John R. Williams
Course Supt.: Doug Palm

18 - R - 6560 - 72

The course is sculptured through the natural beauty of forests, wetlands and rolling hills. Individual, family and corporate memberships available.

| | |
|---|---|
| $$ | |
| Golf Pkgs. | Public |
| Power Carts | Lessons |
| Lounge | Snack Bar |
| Meals | |

## CHEBOYGAN GOLF & COUNTRY CLUB

**CHEBOYGAN, MI (On Old Mackinaw Road, off US 23 N.)**
**Telephone: (616)627-4264 (Tee Times Required)**

Manager: Ed Kelbel Jr.
Head Pro: Ed Kelbel Jr.
Course Supt.: Dan Pillard

18 - R - 6003 - 70

This course is rather unique in that the first nine are Scottish Links style and the second nine are Northern Michigan Hardwoods. It has recently undergone a half-million dollar renovation.

| | |
|---|---|
| $$ | |
| Golf Pkgs. | Public |
| Power Carts | Lessons |
| Lounge | Snack Bar |
| | |

# LAKE TRAIL MOTEL

5400 N. US 23
Oscoda, Michigan 48750

A night in our tastefully decorated V.I.P. section includes the morning Free Press and Contential Breakfast delivered to your room, compliments of the management. Our Lap of Luxury suites are known for their spacious size, a heart shaped jacuzzi-tub for two and enclosed in glamorous mirrored walls. All V.I.P. compliments and splits of cold champagne await your arrival.

- FOUR GOLF COURSES NEARBY -

**On Premise Amenities:**

- 300 feet of sandy beach to stroll and play on , between refreshing dips in clean, cool, blue Lake Huron.
- Tennis court located at the beach's edge.
- Golf practice net.
- Pavillion tent.
- Beautifully manicured green lawns, dotted with picnic tables and bar-b-que grills.
- Basketball court & Shuffleboard.
- In room movies

FOR MORE INFORMATION CALL:

**1-800-843-6007**
TOLL FREE

**(517) 739-2096**
LOCAL

## GOLF PACKAGES

If golf is your passion, or even if you're just a beginner, ***you'll love the variety of play here in the heart of America's summer golf capital.*** We're no more than half an hour from fifteen of the most challenging and scenic golf courses in Michigan. In fact, eight championship courses are right in our backyard so you can tee off within minutes of leaving your room.

Holiday Inn®
OF GAYLORD

I-75 at M-32 Exit 282 Gaylord Michigan 49735

Contact: **Vickie Frost or Daune Weiss**
**Tel:(517) 732-2431**

FOR RESERVATIONS CALL: 1-800-HOLIDAY

## LAKEVIEW HILLS COUNTRY CLUB

**LEXINGTON, MI (On East Peck Road)**
**Clubhouse: (313)359-7333** **Pro Shop: (313)359-8901**

Owners: The Fabbri Family
Manager: Rick Fabbri
Head Pro: Dennis Fabbri
Course Supt.: Mark Murphy

North Course: 18 - R - 6852- 72
South Course: 18 - R - 6290 - 72

| | |
|---|---|
| $$ | Resort |
| Golf Pkgs. | Public |
| Power Carts | Lessons |
| Lounge | Snack Bar |
| Meals | Open All Year |

## LAKEWOOD SHORES GOLF & COUNTRY CLUB

**OSCODA, MI (On Cedar Lake Rd., off Hwy F41)**
**Telephone: (517)739-2073**

Manager: Stan Aldridge
Head Pro: Craig Peters
Course Supt.: Rick York
Architects: Gailes Course - Bob Cupp/Kevin Aldridge
Resort Course - Jerry Matthews

Gailes Course: 18 - R - 6393 - 72
Resort Course: 18 - R - 6511 - 72

| | |
|---|---|
| $$$ | Resort |
| Golf Pkgs. | Public |
| Power Carts | Lessons |
| Lounge | Snack Bar |
| Meals | |

THE PINES

## PINES AT LAKE ISABELLA, THE

**WEIDMAN, MI (On Coldwater Rd, 13 Mi. N/W of Mount Pleasant)**
**Telephone: (517)644-2300 Fax: (517)644-5009**

Owners: Dane Gamble/Joe Schumer
Manager: Mark Holiday
Head Pro: Joe Schumer - PGA
Course Supt.: Dane Gamble
Architect: Bruce Matthews

18 - R - 6300 - 72
Located in central Michigan's lake country. A supurb layout, The Pines is host to Michigan's State Publinks Matchplay Championships.

| | |
|---|---|
| $ | Resort |
| Golf Pkgs. | Public |
| Power Carts | Lessons |
| Lounge | Snack Bar |
| Meals | |

POHLCAT

## POHLCAT CHAMPIONSHIP GOLF COURSE

**MOUNT PLEASANT, MI (At the junction of US #27 & M-20 East)**
**Clubhouse: (517)773-4331 Fax: (517)772-4952**

Manager: John P. Brehm
Head Pro: John Lindeman - PGA
Course Supt.: Roger Barton - USGA
Architect: Dan Pohl - PGA Touring Pro

36 holes: 18 - R - 6877 - 72
18 - Ex. - 3722 - 63

| | |
|---|---|
| $$$ | Resort |
| Golf Pkgs. | Public |
| Power Carts | Lessons |
| Lounge | Snack Bar |
| Meals | Open All Year |

See our full page ad on opposite page.

CHARTER AIR PACKAGES

1ST CorporateAir

Livingston County Airport • Howell, Michigan • 48843

Fly the
**"Pohlcat Express"**

. . . direct to the new Pohlcat 18-hole championship golf course.

Charter air packages currently available from Detroit, Cleveland, Columbus, Cincinnati, Milwaukee, Fort Wayne, Indianapolis, Chicago, Louisville, and Toronto, Canada (Buttonville Airport)

Fly the "Pohlcat Express". We'll pick you up in a catcart and take you directly to the course, while your luggage goes to your Holiday Inn room.

**FOR RESERVATIONS CALL:**

**(517) 772-2905**

*Serving the continental United States and Canada with professional captains committed to unsurpassed service and proud of a 100% uncompromised saftey record.*

# Clarion Hotel & Conference Center

*Ferris State University*

Golf

Enjoy a Golf Weekend, or just call Time Out for a day !

The Clarion's Golf Packages Include:

- Deluxe overnight accommodations for two - one night
- Breakfast for two in Woody's Restaurant
- 18 Holes of Golf for two - with cart - on property at Katke Golf Course or at two additional nearby golf courses.

WEEKDAYS
**from $47.00**
per person plus tax
Sunday thru Thursday nights
Certain conditions apply
Ask for details

WEEKENDS
**from $57.00**
per person plus tax
Friday or Saturday nights
Certain conditions apply
Ask for details

*Katke Golf Club*
*Ferris State University*

FOR RESERVATIONS CONTACT:

***Clarion Hotel & Conference Center***

1005 Perry Street, Big Rapids, Michigan 49307 Tel: (616) 796-4400

## RAISIN RIVER GOLF CLUB

**MONROE, MI (I-75 S. to Exit #15 Munroe - 35 min. from US/Canada border )**
**Telephone: (313)289-3700 or: 1-800-321-9546**

| | |
|---|---|
| $ | |
| Golf Pkgs. | Public |
| Power Carts | Lessons |
| Lounge | Snack Bar |
| Meals | |

Manager: James Spillson
Course Supt.: James Keller
Architect: Charles Maddox

36 Holes: East Course - 18 - R - 6930 - 72
West Course - 18 - R - 6240 - 68

Two completely different golf course designs. Partially wooded with all tees and greens elevated. Greens are bunkered and there is water on 10 holes. Course is maintained to Country Club standards.

STONEBRIDGE
GOLF CLUB

## STONEBRIDGE GOLF CLUB

**ANN ARBOR, MI (On Stonebridge Blvd., off Maple Rd., from Ann Arbor-Saline Rd.)**
**Telephone: (313)429-8383 Fax: (313)994-5973**

| | |
|---|---|
| $$$ | |
| Golf Pkgs. | Public |
| Power Carts | Lessons |
| Lounge | Snack Bar |
| Meals | Open All Year |

Managers: Julie Crouse/Beth Welland
Head Pro: Jeff Graunke
Course Supt.: Rick Bellers
Architect: Arthur Hills

18 - R - 6458 - 72

The feature hole of Stonebridge is the par-4 #10 hole. Eight of the back nine holes have water on them which, along with the wetlands, trees, and man made obstacles make for one of the area's finer, more exciting courses.

# 500 Rounds of GOLF FREE

## Discover 700 New Golf Adventures and Slice Your Green Fees in Half

The 1992 Michigan Golfers Map & Guide names, decribes in detail and locates on maps over 700 golf coures open to the public. Not only an indispensable source of golf travel information, the Golfers Map & Guide also contains certificates entitling two golfers to play 500 rounds of golf for the price of one at over 350 golf courses . . .pays for itself over and over again.

To order send $15.95 plus $2.50 S/H, in U.S. funds, to
RSG Publishing, Inc., P.O. Box 700612, Plymouth, MI 48170

Major Credit Cards Call . . . **1-800-223-5877**

## TAWAS GOLF COURSE

**TAWAS, MI (Just 5 minutes N/W of Tawas, call for specific instructions)**
**Telephone: (517)362-6262 or: 1-800-235-8409**

Manager: Steven Sonoga
Course Supt.: Ted Smith

18 - R - 6065 - 72

A stream flows through this scenic course which is accented by mature hardwoods, cedars and pines. Excellent greens, water hazards and traps makes play interesting but not overly intimidating.

| | |
|---|---|
| $ | |
| Golf Pkgs. | Public |
| Power Carts | Lessons |
| Lounge | Snack Bar |
| Meals | |

## TREETOPS SYLVAN RESORT

**GAYLORD, MI (On Wilkinson Rd., Exit #282 at I-75 East to Wilkinson Rd.)**
**Telephone: (517)732-6711 US Toll Free: 1-800-444-6711**

Manager: Gerald Albert
Dir. of Golf: Rick Smith
Course Supt.: Bruce Wolfrom
Architects: Robert Trent Jones Sr. / Tom Fazio / Rick Smith
18 - R - 7060 - 71 / Robert Trent Jones Sr. - 1987
18 - R - 6871 - 72 / Tom Fazio - 1992

This Robert Trent Jones masterpeice opened in 1987 and has received many State and National awards. A new Tom Fazio course is scheduled to open in June 1992. It will be the first Fazio design in Michigan. Banquet facilities available.

| | |
|---|---|
| $$ | Resort |
| Golf Pkgs. | Public |
| Power Carts | Lessons |
| Lounge | Snack Bar |
| Meals | Open All Year |

DRIVE CAREFULLY
Thank you for visiting ...
*MICHIGAN*
... Come again soon

GOLF CONNECTIONS

# MISSISSIPPI

Pages 89-96

Harrison County Tourism

HOW FAR WOULD YOU GO TO JOIN A CLUB WITH 270 HOLES, A SUBTROPICAL CLIMATE AND NO MEMBERSHIP FEES?
Not far at all, if you head straight south to Mississippi Beach. We're probably the closest winter golf resort to where you are now.
And with all the Canadians we host every winter, you'll feel like you're at your home club. That is, if your home club has 270 challenging holes, fresh seafood, and short sleeve weather.
And after you play golf to your heart's content, get ready to celebrate out on the town. Our world-class restaurants and watering holes are another reason people keep coming back, year after year.
But be sure to bring along Lady Luck for our state regulated casino gambling!
Call today for your Mississippi Beach Golf Planner. Inside, you'll find a value-priced golf package just for you.
Best of all, there's no membership fee.
JOIN THE CELEBRATION!
COME SEA MISSISSIPPI BEACH
1-800-237-9493
P.O. BOX 6128, GULFPORT, MS 39506-6128

1992/93 DIRECTORY

# Golf Vacations

## MISSISSIPPI

Pages 89-96

GOLF CONNECTIONS

## DIAMONDHEAD RESORT COMMUNITY

***" The Best Kept Secret in the South"***

Awaiting you are 36 holes of terrific golf on our Cardinal and Pine courses, nestled within a 6400 acre resort community. We are located 60 miles from NewOrleans, LA.

***DISCOVER DIAMONDHEAD FOR GOLF AT ITS BEST!***

Diamondhead also offers other amenities such as Tennis World, Country Club, Yacht Club and Marina, Airport, numerous parks and pools.

**- GOLF PACKAGES -**

**3 DAYS / 2 NIGHTS. . . $167.96 Per Person**

• Double Occupancy • Tax not included • Rates subject to change

INCLUDES •Two nights lodging• 18 holes of golf per day • Shared golf cart (18 holes per day) • Food & Beverage Allowance

**** SPECIAL MONTHLY RATES AVAILABLE ****

Century 21 Condo Rentals 1-800-221-2423 (USA & Canada)
Diamondhead Inn 1-800-647-9550 (USA & Canada)
Lanai Village Condo Rentals 1-800-345-7915 (USA & Canada)

**FOR FREE BROCHURE WRITE: DIAMONDHEAD COUNTRY CLUB**
**7600 COUNTRY CLUB CIRCLE, BAY ST. LOUIS, MS 39520**

## DIAMONDHEAD COUNTRY CLUB

**BAY ST. LOUIS, MS (On Country Club Circle)**
**Telephone: (601)255-2525**

General Manager: Paul Montjoy
Head Pro: Phil Hill
Course Supt.: Warren Wittenburg

Cardinal Course: 18 - R - 6163 - 72
Rating: Men's - 70.6, Ladies' - 68.9
Pine Course: 18 - R - 6421 - 72
Rating: Men's - 71.7, Ladies' - 71.1

| | |
|---|---|
| $$ | Resort |
| Golf Packages | Public |
| Power Carts | Lessons |
| Lounge | Snack Bar |
| Meals | Open All Year |

## EDGEWATER BAY GOLF COURSE

**BILOXI, MS (On Pass Road, at the Edgewater Mall)**
**Telephone: (601)388-9670 Fax: (601)388-9670**

Gen Mgr: Art Mitchell
Head Pro: George White

18 - R - 6196 - 71

This course is heavily wooded with large oak trees. Six holes overlook Back Bay Biloxi. FORMERLY RAINBOW GOLF CLUB.1

| | |
|---|---|
| $ | |
| Golf Pkgs. | Public |
| Power Carts | Lessons |
| Lounge | Snack Bar |
| | Open All Year |

## ROYAL GULF HILLS RESORT & COUNTRY CLUB

**OCEAN SPRINGS, MS (I-90 exit 50, S. 3 MI. to Royal Gulf Hills entrance)**
**Telephone: (601)875-4211 Fax: (601)872-3504**
**US & Ontario Toll Free: 1-800-638-4902**

Manager: Robert Thompson
Head Pro: Dave Hull
Course Supt.: Jimmy Fayard

18 - R - 6300 - 71

Heavily wooded, rolling fairways, water comes into play on several holes. Major refurbishing of the course was completed in September 1989.

| | |
|---|---|
| $$ | Resort |
| Golf Pkgs. | Public |
| Power Carts | Lessons |
| Lounge | Snack Bar |
| Meals | Open All Year |

## SUNKIST COUNTRY CLUB

**BILOXI, MS (Just off Popps Ferry Bridge, 2 Mi. N. of Hwy. 90)**
**Office: (601)388-3201 Pro Shop: (601)388-3961**

18 - R - 6276 - 72

Wooded, rolling fairways blended with 17 bunkers, well placed water hazards, and excellent well maintained turf.

| | |
|---|---|
| $$ | |
| Golf Pkgs. | Public |
| Power Carts | Lessons |
| Lounge | Snack Bar |
| | Open All Year |

Pine island Golf Course

## PINE ISLAND GOLF CLUB

**OCEAN SPRINGS, MS. (Hwy. 90, S. on Henshaw Rd., R. at 1st. stop, then 1st. L.)**
**Telephone: (601)875-1674 Fax: (601)875-0395**

Director of Golf: Martin Reeves
Head Pro:Luke Rodney
Course Supt.: Tony Belson
Designer: Pete Dye

18 - R - 6310 - 71

Built on three islands this course offers beautiful scenery, abundant wildlife and challenging golf. It is well manicured with typical Pete Dye greens and tees.

| | |
|---|---|
| $$ | |
| Golf Pkgs. | Public |
| Power Carts | Lessons |
| Lounge | Snack Bar |
| | Open All Year |

St. Andrews ON THE GULF

## ST. ANDREWS COUNTRY CLUB

**OCEAN SPRINGS, MS (1.5 Mi. E. of Hospital to Hanshaw Rd., Turn R. follow signs)**
**Telephone: (601)875-7730 Fax: (601)875-6126**

Director of Golf: Martin Reeves
Manager: Jane Reeves
Head Pro: Don Barbato
Course Supt.: Michael Herring

18 - R - 6037 - 72

This course interweaves with a beautiful St. Andrews subdivision. The 13th. green offers a wonderful view of the Gulf and Barrier Islands. Hole #13 is also the famous "Lighthouse Hole". Clubhouse has been recently remodelled.

| | |
|---|---|
| $$ | |
| Golf Pkgs. | Public |
| Power Carts | Lessons |
| Lounge | Snack Bar |
| | Open All Year |

TRAMARK
GOLF COURSE

## TRAMARK GOLF COURSE

**GULFPORT, MS (3 Mi. N of the airport, take Hewes Ave. off Hwy 90 follow the signs)**
**Telephone: (601)863-7808**

Owner/Pro: Billy Applewhite
Teaching Pro: Sheryl Applewhite
Assistant: Mark Applewhite

18 - R - 6350 - 72

Dogleg fairways will challenge your concentration.A few water hazards and sand traps create interesting shots into rolling greens.

| | |
|---|---|
| $ | |
| Golf Pkgs. | Public |
| Power Carts | Lessons |
| | Snack Bar |
| Meals | Open All Year |

# Holiday Inn

**Stay with someone you know.**

GREAT GOLF PACKAGES

### Holiday Inn - Biloxi

BEACHFRONT (COLISEUM)
2400 Beach Blvd. Biloxi, MS 39531

**(601)338-3551** or
**1-800-441-0882** (US Toll Free)

starting at
**3 Days / 2 Nights**

**$117.00** - Sept. 8/92 to Jan. 31/93
**$133.00** - Feb. 1/93 to May 23/93

---

### Holiday Inn - Gulfport

BEACHFRONT
1600 East Beach, Gulfport, MS 39501

**(601)864-4310** or
**1-800-441-0887** (US Toll Free)

starting at
**3 Days / 2 Nights**

**$116.00** - Sept. 8/92 to Jan. 31/93
**$125.00** - Feb. 1/93 to May 23/93

---

### Holiday Inn - Gulfport

I-10 / US 49
9415 Hwy. 49 Gulfport, MS 39502

**(601)868-8200** or
**1-800-441-0892** (US Toll Free)

starting at
**3 Days / 2 Nights**

**$111.00** - Sept. 8/92 to Jan. 31/93
**$119.00** - Feb. 1/93 to May 23/93

ALL PACKAGES INCLUDE:
A choice of twelve golf courses, a golf cap, $20.00 food and beverage allowance, and green fees with tee times prearranged by the golf coordinator.
(Rates are per person / double occupancy)

Gulfshores, Inc.
HOTEL MANAGEMENT COMPANY

## Holiday Inn Hotels of the MISSISSIPPI GULF COAST

Owned by Gulfshores, Inc.
Operated under license from Holiday Inns, Inc.

# Gulf Beach

**• RESORT • HOTEL •**

**Featuring . . .**

***NANCY FOBES***
***THE GOLF GAL FROM BILOXI***

There are many good hotels on the Mississippi Gulf Coast, but only the GULF BEACH has Nancy Fobes.

For years, Nancy has been arranging and planning golf vacations for visiting golfers to the Gulf Coast and year after year her golf groups keep coming back for more. What makes her golf packages so special is the little extra effort she adds.

She has an excellent working knowledge and relationship with all the courses on the Gulf. Not only will she make all the tee times for your group and have everything ready for you the moment you walk through the door . . . if asked, she will even fill in for a missing golfer to complete a foursome.

When GOLF CONNECTIONS first visited the Mississippi Gulf Coast a number of years ago we had the opportunity to play with this talented and avid golfer. She is such good company on the course, you just don't notice the score until its time to add it all up. It is only then that you realize just how well this gal plays and how badly she has beaten you. No wonder a return engagement is in order (along with a renegotiation of strokes given on the first tee).

Besides Arnold Palmer, Nancy's idols include ELVIS, Bobby Knight and Mickey Mouse. Maybe if you can get her to talk about them on the golf course, you might have a chance of defeating her.

For great golf
on the
MISSISSIPPI GULF COAST

Contact: Nancy Fobes
Gulf Beach Hotel

2428 Beach Blvd. Biloxi MS 39531
Tel: (601)385-5555 or 1-800-323-9164

# SHONEY'S INN

***Shoney's Inn Of Gulfport*** *is convenient to all places you will want to see. We're located in the center of a colorful world of shrimp fleets, marine life, sparkling sand beaches, exciting night life, deep sea fishing and casino cruise ships.*

**Includes:** • 18 Holes of Golf
- Shoney's Breakfast & Fruit Bar
- Free HBO with Remote Control
- Complimentary Coffee
- No Charge for Local Telephone Calls
- Your choice of Queen Size or Two Double Beds
- Rainy Day Indoor Golf Clinic

***$40.00***

(pp/per night - dbl. occ. excluding taxes)

Rates available for additional golfers.
Surcharge on some courses.
Credit allowed for non-golfers

## *GOLF PACKAGES*

(Feb.1,1992 - May 31,1993)

SHONEY'S INN

For reservations & information on ALL Shoney's Inns
CALL TOLL FREE
U.S.A.: **1-800-222-2222**
CANADA: **1-800-223-4667**

9375 HIGHWAY 49, GULFPORT, MISSISSIPPI (601) 868-8500

---

# La Linda

**MOTOR INN**

- Air Conditioning - Heat
- Direct Dial Telephones
- Commercial Rates
- Cable TV / Free HBO
- Kitchenettes
- Swimming Pool
- Lounge
- Near Keesler AFB

• GOLF PACKAGES •

1836 Beach Blvd. Biloxi, MS 39531 **Tel: (601)388-4621**

GOLF CONNECTIONS

# NEW YORK

Pages 97-104

Bristol Harbour Golf Course

1992/93 DIRECTORY

# Golf Vacations

## NEW YORK

Pages 97-104

GOLF CONNECTIONS

Batavia CC

## BATAVIA COUNTRY CLUB

**BATAVIA, NY (On Batavia-Bryon Rd., from thruway exit 48 to Main St. to Rte. 33)**
**Telephone: (716)343-7600**

Manager: Karen L. Pompa
Course Supt.: William McDonald

18 - R - 7134 - 72

Golf Packages - Monday, Wednesday and Friday during the season. Includes green fees, cart and dinner for two.

| | |
|---|---|
| $ | |
| Golf Pkgs. | Public |
| Power Carts | Lessons |
| Lounge | Snack Bar |
| Meals | |

BLUE HERON HILLS
Country Club

- 25 MINUTES FROM THE CITY OF ROCHESTER -

## BLUE HERON HILLS COUNTRY CLUB

**MACEDON, NY (On Country Club Dr., from Canadaigua Rd., from Granada Pkwy.)**
**Telephone: (315)986-2007 Fax: (716)546-5433**

Manager: Nelson B. Leenhouts
Head Pro: Chuck Salitan
Course Supt.: Dan DeGraff
Architect: Dick Bator

18 - R - 5970 - 71
This course offers championship playing conditions with bent grass fairways and scenic forever wild surroundings. Home of the Hillside Skins Challenge.

| | |
|---|---|
| $$ | |
| | Public |
| Power Carts | Lessons |
| Lounge | Snack Bar |
| Meals | |

BRISTOL HARBOUR

*On Canandaigua Lake*

At the BRISTOL HARBOUR GOLF CLUB in Canadaigua, NY you will experience one of Western New York's most talked about golf courses.

This 6700-yard championship course, designed by Robert Trent Jones in 1972, is nestled in the breathtaking Bristol Hills overlooking Canadaigua Lake . . . the gem of the Finger Lakes.

A superb test of golf, the course combines natural settings with an outstanding sequence of holes. The photo that graces the Title Page of this New York section is an example of what you will find at BRISTOL HARBOUR.

Perhaps the most underated hole on the course is #11, a par 3 that plays 148 yards from the reds, 173 yards from the whites and 216 yards from the blues . . .

The green is diagonal with bunkers protecting the right front and left rear. Club selection is the key and a par here usually picks up one to two strokes on the field.

Keeping your mind on your game can be difficult as this hole offers a most spectacular view of Canadaigua Lake, one of many you will experience as you play your round.

BRISTOL HARBOUR offers many different golf packages with accommodations in their Lakeside Condominiums or Lakeside Townhomes.

To find out more or to book your reservations, just call 1-800-288-8248 and . . . experience the difference !!!

## BRISTOL HARBOUR GOLF CLUB

**CANANDAIGUA, NY (Rte. 332 S. to Rte 21 S. follow signs to Bristol Harbour)**
**Office: 1-800-288-8248 Pro Shop: (716)396-2460**

Manager: Mark Knickerbocker
Head Pro: Suellen Northrup
Course Supt.: Ken Leach
Architect: Robert Trent Jones

18 - R - 6100 - 72
Course Record of 67 held by Jack Nicklaus.
Host of the 1992 New York State Men's Mid-Amateur.

| | |
|---|---|
| $$ | Resort |
| Golf Pkgs. | |
| Power Carts | Lessons |
| Lounge | Snack Bar |
| Meals | |

## CHESTNUT HILL COUNTRY CLUB

**DARIEN, NY. (NY State Thruway I-90, to exit 48A, 5 Mi. S on Rte. #77)**
**Clubhouse:(716)547-9699 Pro Shop: (716)547-3613**

Manager: Chris Protos
Head Pro: William Kay
Course Supt.: Michael Kaminski

18 - R - 6400 - 72
Rating: Men's - 70.2, Ladies' - 69.6

An all weather course at competitive prices. Among the best greens in Western New York. Seniors Specials Monday to Friday.

| | |
|---|---|
| $ | |
| Golf Pkgs. | Public |
| Power Carts | Lessons |
| Lounge | Snack Bar |
| Meals | |

## TERRY HILLS GOLF COURSE

**BATAVIA, NY. (On Rte. 33, 10 Min. from N.Y. State Thruway exit #48)**
**Telephone: (716)343-0860 Toll Free: 1-800-825-8633**
(US and Canada)

President: Joseph Rotondo
Dir. of Golf: Nicholas J. Rotondo
Architect: Ed Ault

18 - R - 6038 - 72

18 exciting holes with watered fairways.Tee times taken seven days a week - call in advance. "The best kept secret in Western New York"

| | |
|---|---|
| $$ | |
| | Public |
| Power Carts | Lessons |
| Lounge | Snack Bar |
| Meals | |

## HOLIDAY VALLEY RESORT

**ELLICOTTVILLE, NY. (On Rte. 219, 45 Mi. S. of I-90, in Buffalo)**
**Resort: (716)699-2345 Pro Shop: (716)699-2346**

Head Pro: Dick Eaton
Course Supt.: Don Wagner

18 - R - 6555 - 72
Rating: Men's - 71, Ladies' - 74

Spectacular scenery and variety makes this one of the most exciting courses in Western New York. Plenty of water, traps and natural hazards add to the challenge.

| | |
|---|---|
| $$ | Resort |
| Golf Pkgs. | Public |
| Power Carts | Lessons |
| Lounge | Snack Bar |
| Meals | Open All Year |

## PEEK'N PEAK RESORT & CONFERENCE CENTER

**CLYMER, NY (On Ye Olde Rd., I-90 to Rte. 17, exit at Findlay Lake)**
**Telephone: (716)355-4141**

General Manger: John Gallagher
Head Pro: Steve Card - PGA

18 - R - 6260 - 72 Rating: Men's - 69, Ladies' - 72

A natural playground amidst one of Western New York's most beautiful settings.

| | |
|---|---|
| $$ | Resort |
| Golf Pkgs. | Public |
| Power Carts | Lessons |
| Lounge | Snack Bar |
| Meals | Open All Year |

## THOUSAND ISLANDS GOLF CLUB

**WELLESLEY ISLAND EAST, NY (Exit 51 off Route 81 to Wellesley Island E.)**

**Telephone: (315)482-9454** **Fax: (315)482-9321**

Owner/Manager: Doug Horton
Head Pro: Frank Picone
Course Supt.: Richard Shaver
Architect: Seth Reiner

18 - R - 5997 - 72

Scottish Links Style. Rolling hills, scenic holes bordering the St. Lawrence River.

| | |
|---|---|
| $ | |
| Golf Pkgs. | Public |
| Power Carts | Lessons |
| Lounge | Snack Bar |
| Meals | |

DRIVE CAREFULLY
Thank you for visiting . . .
NEW YORK
. . . Come again soon

GOLF CONNECTIONS

# NORTH CAROLINA

Pages 105-128

Pinehurst Area CVB

1992/93 DIRECTORY

# *Golf Vacations*

# NORTH CAROLINA

Pages 105-128

GOLF CONNECTIONS

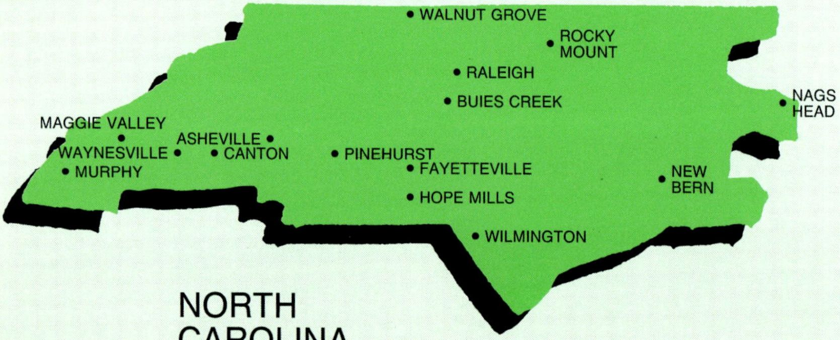


NORTH CAROLINA

## CHEROKEE HILLS GOLF COURSE

**MURPHY, NC. (In Murphy turn R. at McDonalds , go 3 Mi.)**
**Telephone: (704)837-5853     US Toll Free: 1-800-334-3905**

Owner: Roy Wells
Head Pro: Gary Toth
Course Supt.: James Cook

18 - R - 6500 - 72

The course has a great layout. Hilly with nice greens and beautiful views.

| | |
|---|---|
| $$ | Resort |
| Golf Pkgs. | Public |
| Power Carts | Lessons |
| | Snack Bar |
| | Open All Year |

## CYPRESS LAKES GOLF COURSE

**HOPE MILLS, NC. (Off I-95 Exit 41, follow signs)**
**Telephone: (919)483-0359     Fax: (919)323-5806**

Owner: Al Prewitt
Manager: Tom Prewitt
Head Pro: Ken Robertson - PGA
Course Supt.: Arden Smith
Architect: L.B. Floyd
18 - R - 6640 - 72
Home of the "Floyds". . . . Ray Floyd - 1986 US Open Champ, sister Marlene - Touring Pro, and dad L.B. Cypress Lakes has earned its right as one of the region's finest courses, with lush Bermuda fairways and bent grass greens.

| | |
|---|---|
| $$ | |
| Golf Pkgs. | Public |
| Power Carts | Lessons |
| Lounge | Snack Bar |
| Meals | Open All Year |

## EMERALD GOLF CLUB, THE

**NEW BERN, NC. (Hwy. 70 W. to Glenburnie Rd. exit, L. one block, turn R.)**
**Telephone: (919)633-4440**

Owner/Mgr.: David S. Woodruff
Dir. of Golf: Jerry Briele
Course Supt.: Jim Lanier
Architect: Rees Jones

18 - R - 6900 - 72
Voted by *Golf Week Magazine* one of the top 50 development courses in the Southeast. FORMERLY GREENBRIER GOLF CLUB.

| | |
|---|---|
| $$$ | Resort |
| Golf Pkgs. | Public |
| Power Carts | Lessons |
| Lounge | Snack Bar |
| | Open All Year |

## CHEVIOT HILLS GOLF COURSE

**RALEIGH, NC. (On US 1 N. of Raleigh, 1 Mi. N. of Plantation Inn, )**
**Telephone: (919)876-9920**

Owner: Bill Edwards
Head Pro: J. Percy Card
Course Supt.: J. Ray Autry
Architect: Gene Hamm

18 - R - 6500 - 71

Interesting, scenic course requiring many different shots over rolling countryside similar to Cheviot Hills in Scotland (after which it was named). Bent grass greens.

| | |
|---|---|
| $ | |
| | Public |
| Power Carts | Lessons |
| | Snack Bar |
| | Open All Year |

# COURTYARD
Marriott

## *STAY-N-PLAY at the BEST in FAYETTEVILLE*

**GOLF PACKAGES INCLUDE:**

- Deluxe overnight accommodations. Each room features in-room coffee service, remote control color television with free HBO, CNN, & ESPN, AM/FM clock radio and seperate seating area.
- Continental breakfast in our full service restaurant
- Daily green and cart fees for 18 holes • Preferred tee times
- Courtyard with Gazebo and outdoor pool
- Indoor whirlpool and exercise room • Cozy lounge

**PARTICIPATING COURSES:**

| COURSE | ARCHITECT | YARDS | GREENS | MILES FROM HOTEL |
|---|---|---|---|---|
| Baywood | S. Gooden | 6763 | Bent | 15 |
| Carolina Lakes | R. Ruleorwitz | 6377 | Bent | 17 |
| Cypress Lakes | L.B. Floyd | 7240 | Bent | 15 |
| *Deercroft | G. Didley | 6745 | Bent | 35 |
| Gates Four C.C. | W. Byrd | 7011 | Bent | 10 |
| Keith Hills C.C. | E. Maples | 6660 | Bermuda | 30 |
| King's Grant | J. Holmes | 6750 | Bent | 9 |
| Lakewood C.C. | R.T. Burney | 6708 | Bent | 33 |
| *Legacy Golf Links | J. Nicklaus II | 6989 | Bent | 31 |
| Pirates Ridge | H. Stegal | 6000 | Bermuda | 13 |
| *The Pit | D. Maples | 6600 | Bent | 37 |
| *Woodlake C.C. | E. & D. Maples | 7045 | Bent | 25 |

* Surcharge at these courses

**COURTYARD by Marriott**

is easily accessible from major Interstates and is located adjacent to outlet malls, restaurants and movie theaters.

CALL OUR SALES DEPARTMENT
FOR RESERVATIONS

**(919)487-5557**

4192 Sycamore Dairy Road, Fayetteville, North Carolina 28303

## GREAT SMOKIES HILTON RESORT & C. CENTER

**ASHEVILLE, NC. (1.5 Mi. W. of Asheville, I-240 W., 3 Mi. N. of I-26)**
**Telephone: (704)254-3211 Toll Free: 1-800-HILTONS**

Manager: Wayne Tabor
Head Pro: Ervin Ingle
Course Supt.: Ed Downs
Architect: Willie B. Lewis

18 - R - 5300 - 70

Located on 120 Mountain Acres. The "Ridgerunner"offers a challenging round with tight fairways, water hazards on 9 holes and lots of vertical change.

| | |
|---|---|
| $$ | Resort |
| Golf Pkgs. | Public |
| Power Carts | Lessons |
| Lounge | Snack Bar |
| Meals | Open All Year |

## HEMLOCK GOLF CLUB

**WALNUT COVE, NC. (On Power Dam Rd., off Hwy. 89, 3 Mi. N. of Walnut Cove)**
**Telephone: (919)591-7934**

Owners/Mgrs.: Keith & Kadren Robertson
Head Pro: Tommy Zigler
Course Supt.: Keith Robertson
Architect: Orell Robertson

18 - R - 5482 - 70

This course, adjacent to the Dan River, has well kept greens, and is very hilly with nice views.

| | |
|---|---|
| $ | |
| | Public |
| Power Carts | Lessons |
| | Snack Bar |
| | Open All Year |

## KEITH HILLS COUNTRY CLUB

**BUIES CREEK, NC. (I-95 S. to Hwy 421, 10 Mi. W. to Buies Creek)**
**Telephone: (919)893-5051**

Manager: Cad Upchurch
Course Supt.: John Williams
Architect: Ellis Maples

18 - R - 6600 - 72

Keith Hills is consistently rated in North Carolina's top 30 golf courses.

| | |
|---|---|
| $$ | |
| Golf Pkgs. | Public |
| Power Carts | |
| | Snack Bar |
| | Open All Year |

KING'S GRANT
GOLF & COUNTRY CLUB

## KING'S GRANT GOLF & COUNTRY CLUB

**FAYETTEVILLE, NC (On Hwy. 401 N., 1/2 mi. past Methodist College on the left.)**
**Telephone: (919)630-1111 Fax: (919)630-2122**

General Manager: John M. Rose, Jr.
Head Pro: Robert Wilson
Course Supt.: Peter Horn
Architect: Jim Holmes

18 - R - 5863 - 72

Not overpowering in distance, but accuracy is important. A shot maker's course with water on holes 10 to 18. Varying elevation and terrain and bent grass greens.

| | |
|---|---|
| $$$ | |
| Golf Pkgs. | Public |
| Power Carts | Lessons |
| | Snack Bar |
| | Open All Year |

Maggie Valley Resort

## MAGGIE VALLEY RESORT & COUNTRY CLUB

**MAGGIE VALLEY, NC. (6 Mi. S. of I-40, 1/2 Mi. from intersection of 276 & 19)**
**Telephone: (704)926-1616 US Toll Free: 1-800-438-3861**

| | |
|---|---|
| $$ | Resort |
| Golf Pkgs. | Public |
| Power Carts | Lessons |
| Lounge | Snack Bar |
| Meals | Open All Year |

Manager: Russ Smith
Head Pro: Ted Staats
Course Supt.: Mike Stamey
Architect: Ross Prevost

18 - R - 6004 - 71
Breathtaking scenery surrounds this challenging course located in the Great Smoky and Blue Ridge Mountains. Headquarters of the Professional Golf School of America. Outstanding cuisine and atmosphere.

## NAGS HEAD GOLF LINKS

**NAGS HEAD, NC. (On US 158 Bypass at Milepost 15, off Hwy. 64 E.)**
**Telephone: (919)441-8073**

| | |
|---|---|
| $$$ | Resort |
| Golf Pkgs. | Public |
| Power Carts | Lessons |
| Lounge | Snack Bar |
| Meals | Open All Year |

Owner/Mgr.: Andrew Ammons
Head Pro: Phill Hunt
Course Supt.: Gary Bell
Architect: Jerry Turner & Associates

18 - R - 5717 - 71

True links course with ten water holes and five holes along Roanoke Sound. Superbly manicured fairways and bent grass greens.

## SPRINGDALE COUNTRY CLUB

**CANTON, NC. (Hwy. 110 S. from Canton to US 276, S. 6 Mi.)**
**Telephone: (704)235-8451**

Owner/Mgr.: G. Fredrick Tingle
Course Supt.: Bob Feser
Architect: Joe Holmes

18 - R - 6812 - 72

A creek meanders through the hilly front and flat back of this golf course. Excellent accommodations, good food, with unique golf packages, including a personal cart for each twosome.

| | |
|---|---|
| $$ | Resort |
| Golf Pkgs. | Public |
| Power Carts | |
| Lounge | Snack Bar |
| Meals | Open All Year |

## WAYNESVILLE COUNTRY CLUB INN

**WAYNESVILLE, NC. (I-40 to exit 20, to W. Waynesville exit, turn L. follow signs)**
**Telephone: (704)456-3551**

Owner/Mgr.: Reimar K. Steffen
Head Pro: Duane Page
Course Supt.: Caney Kilby
Architects: John Drake/Tom Jackson

18 - R - 6050 - 70
Also another 9 holes. Bent grass greens and scenic views over rolling fairways, through brooks and streams. Good golf, good friends, good times.

| | |
|---|---|
| $$ | Resort |
| Golf Pkgs. | Public |
| Power Carts | Lessons |
| Lounge | Snack Bar |
| Meals | Open All Year |

## *Experience "Golf's Grandest Era"*

What exactly is it that made the Pinehurst Area synonymous with the game of golf? Is it the more than 30 superb championship courses, some of which are the most highly rated in the world? Is it the fact that Pinehurst is the home of the PGA / World Golf Hall of Fame? Or is it because professional golfers and celebrities alike have, for more than eighty years, held Pinehurst Area golf in such high regard?

For many, it's all these things and more that count for Pinehurst's standing in the world of golf and perhaps it can be summarized in one word . . . ***tradition.***

Nestled in the Sandhills of North Carolina among quaint villages and towns, the Pinehurst Area is steeped in the traditions that indeed epitomize golf's grandest era.

This was an era when legends were born and grew, with names like Nelson, Zaharias, Hagen, Jones, Hogan, Snead and Palmer. It was a time of craftmanship and pride in handmade golf clubs called by such personable names as niblicks, brassies, mashies and spoons. And while competition may have been fierce, it was competition in the true spirit of sport. Because this was a time of warmth, friendship and goodwill.

Every golfer should experience "Golf's Grandest Era" at least once in their lifetime. This extraordinary time and feeling still exists today among Pinehurst Area's rolling hills and spectacular, challenging courses.

Just contact the Pinehurst Area Convention & Visitors Bureau.
P.O. Box 2270, Southern Pines, NC 28388
Tel: (919) 692-3330 or 1-800-346-5362 Fax: (919)692-0619

*Picture the perfect day - you and your friends experiencing a fun-filled, challenging round of golf on a fabulous 18 hole course; rolling hills of fine turf, designed by the renowned architect, Gene Hamm. The par 72 championship course demanding accuracy and full use of avariety of clubs.*

*Located just minutes west of the Pinehurst traffic circle, Beacon Ridge Golf & Country Club is fast becoming one of the area's most popular courses, challenging to the skilled and beginning golfer alike.*

*Guest Services at Beacon Ridge include:*

- *Grill/lounge*
- *Swimming pool*
- *Tennis courts*
- *1000-acre lake*
- *Colour Television*
- *Putting and chipping greens*
- *Driving range*

*Beacon Ridge golf villas are available in one (capacity 4 persons) or two bedroom suites (capacity 6 persons) with fully equipped kitchens as well as single guest units (capacity 2 persons).*

## Golf Packages

*Discounted green fees are available to our guests on the Beacon Ridge golf course. Tee times may also be arranged at other areas courses. Special golf packages may be arranged.*

*For more information write: P.O. Box 629, West End, NC 27376 or call: (919) 673-7700 • 1-800-762-1107*

# BEACON RIDGE COUNTRY CLUB

**WEST END, NC (On Longleaf Drive)**
**Telephone: (919)673-2950**

Head Pro: Kent Shumate
Architect: Gene Hamm

18 - R - 6511 - 72 Rating: Men's - 70.6, Ladies - N/A

Trees, sand, water and distance combine to test the skills of the most seasoned players while club players are still offered a fair and delightful opportunity to capitalize on well-struck golf shots.

| | |
|---|---|
| $$ | Resort |
| Golf Pkgs. | Public |
| Power Carts | Lessons |
| Lounge | Snack Bar |
| Meals | Open All Year |

FOXFIRE

*Resort & Country Club*

## FOXFIRE RESORT & COUNTRY CLUB

**PINEHURST, NC. (On Hoffman Rd.)**
**Telephone: (919)295-4563**

Head Pro: Tom Graber
Architect: Gene Hamm

36 holes: East course: 18 - R - 6851 - 72
Rating: Men's - 72.4, Ladies' - 70.3
West course: 18 - R - 6741 - 72
Rating: Men's - 72.4, Ladies' - 70.3
Bermuda fairways and bent grass greens.

| | |
|---|---|
| $$ | Resort |
| Golf Pkgs. | Public |
| Power Carts | Lessons |
| Lounge | Snack Bar |
| Meals | Open All Year |

# Hampton Inn

## Southern Pines / Pinehurst North Carolina

*One of Pinehurst Area's newest properties. One hundred and twenty -six rooms, all comfortably decorated. And the hotel's convenient location provides easy access to all area attractions.*

**GREAT GOLF PACKAGES AT ECONOMICAL RATES !**

*Includes:*

- *Daily green fees*
- *Deluxe accommodations*
- *Continental breakfast*
- *Outdoor pool*
- *Color TV, cable, HBO, ESPN & CNN*
- *Free local phone calls*
- *Guest laundry*

**OVER 30 CHAMPIONSHIP COURSES**

**1-800-333-9266**

Hampton Inn
*U.S. 1, South*
*Southern Pines, NC 28387*
*Local Tel:(919) 692-9266*

*Par 4 Par Exchange Rate February 1993*

Hyland Hills
GOLF CLUB

## HYLAND HILLS GOLF CLUB

**SOUTHERN PINES, NC (On US #1 North)**
**Telephone: (919)692-3752 Fax: (919)692-2765**

Manager: Claude Pardue
Head Pro: Doug Thompson
Course Supt.: Andy Apple
Architect: Tom Jackson

18 - R - 6348 - 72
The highest point of golf in the Pinehurst Area. Located on one of the highest elevations in the region. Tall pines, sparkling blue water and spacious vistas make Hyland Hills an exceptional place to play golf.

| | |
|---|---|
| $$ | Resort |
| Golf Pkgs. | Public |
| Power Carts | Lessons |
| Lounge | Snack Bar |
| Meals | Open All Year |

Legacy
GOLF LINKS

## LEGACY GOLF LINKS

**ABERDEEN, NC (On US Hwy. 15-501 S., off Us #1 S.)**
**Telephone: (919)944-8825 Fax: (919)944-9416**

Owner: Club Development Associates
Head Pro: Danny Barrett
Course Supt.: Peter Dejak
Architect: Jack Nicklaus II

18 - R - 6477 - 72
Golden Bear design. Fully appointed clubhouse, golf shop, club and shoe valet service, day lockers. Legacy's level of maintenance is consistant with the most prestigious private clubs in the area.

| | |
|---|---|
| $$$ | Resort |
| Golf Pkgs. | Public |
| Power Carts | Lessons |
| Lounge | Snack Bar |
| Meals | Open All Year |

THE CLUB AT LONGLEAF

## LONGLEAF, THE CLUB AT

**PINEHURST, NC (On Midland Rd.)**
**Telephone: (919)692-6100**

Head Pro: Scott Brazaski
Architect: Dan Maples

18 - R - 6513 - 71
Rating: Men's - 69.7, Ladies' - N/A

| | |
|---|---|
| $$$ | |
| Golf Pkgs. | Public |
| Power Carts | Lessons |
| Lounge | Snack Bar |
| Meals | Open All Year |

mid pines resort

Mid Pines Resort

## MID PINES RESORT

**SOUTHERN PINES, NC. (US 1 to exits 2 and 22, 1/4 Mi. on Rte. 2, entrance on L.)**
**Telephone: (919)692-2114 Toll Free: 1-800-323-2114**

Dir. of Sales/Mktg.: Helen Downie
Head Pro: Chip King
Architect: Donald Ross

18 - R - 6515 - 72
Rating: Men's - 71.4, Ladies' - 72.3

| | |
|---|---|
| $$ | Resort |
| Golf Pkgs. | Public |
| Power Carts | Lessons |
| Lounge | Snack Bar |
| Meals | Open All Year |

the Pit

## PIT GOLF LINKS, THE

**PINEHURST, NC (On Hwy. #5)**
**Telephone: (919)944-1600**

Head Pro: Eddie Cox
Architect: Dan Maples

18 - R - 6600 - 72
Rating: Men's - 71.8 - Ladies' - N/A

Rated one of the top 50 courses open to the public. *Golf Digest 1988*

| | |
|---|---|
| $$$ | |
| Golf Pkgs. | Public |
| Power Carts | Lessons |
| Lounge | Snack Bar |
| Meals | Open All Year |

TALAMORE
AT • PINEHURST

## TALAMORE AT PINEHURST

**SOUTHERN PINES, NC (On Midland Rd.)**
**Telephone: (919)692-5884 Fax: (919)692-4421**

Owner: Talamore Management Group
General Manager: John Musto
Head Pro: John McDougald
Course Supt.: Chandler Masters
Architect: Rees Jones
18 - R - 6293 - 71

Golf Digest Architectural Commitee nomination for 1991-1992 best new public course. This course features 123 bunkers and LLAMA CADDIES.

| | |
|---|---|
| $$$ | |
| Golf Pkgs. | Public |
| Power Carts | Lessons |
| | Snack Bar |
| | Open All Year |

## RIVERSIDE COUNTRY CLUB

**HIGH FALLS, NC (On North Carolina Hwy. #22, 20 mi. N. of Pinehurst)**
**Telephone: (919)464-3686**

President: Dock G. Smith, Jr.
Architect: Porter Gibson

18 - R - 6159 - 72
Rating: Men's - 72.5, Ladies' - N/A

| | |
|---|---|
| $ | |
| Golf Pkgs. | Public |
| Power Carts | |
| | Snack Bar |
| Meals | Open All Year |

WOODLAKE
COUNTRY CLUB

## WOODLAKE COUNTRY CLUB

**VASS, NC (#1 S. to Vass L. at flashing light on Rte. 1001, follow the signs)**
**Telephone: (919)245-4031 US Toll Free: 1-800-334-1126**

General Manager: Martha Tattersall
Head Pro: Stuart Taylor
Course Supt.: Randy Dallas
Architects: Ellis & Dan Maples

18 - R - 7002 - 72
Rating: Men's - 73.4, Ladies' - 69.5
Woodlake has a new 9 hole - 3422 yard par 36 course.
They also have an aquatic driving range.

| | |
|---|---|
| $$$ | |
| Golf Pkgs. | Public |
| Power Carts | Lessons |
| Lounge | Snack Bar |
| Meals | Open All Year |

*Beau Rivage Plantation*

## BEAU RIVAGE PLANTATION

**WILMINGTON, NC (On. Hwy. #421, 7 Mi. S. of Wilmington)**
**Telephone: (919)392-9021 Toll Free: 1-800-628-7080**

Owners: Eddie & Peggy Lewis
Head Pro: Tom Willock
Course Supt.: David Carriker

18 - R - 6166 - 72

Natural rolling hills with bent grass greens and paved cart paths. Beau Rivage offers on-site deluxe accommodations with private balcony and a view of the course.

| | |
|---|---|
| $$ | Resort |
| Golf Pkgs. | Public |
| Power Carts | Lessons |
| Lounge | Snack Bar |
| Meals | Open All Year |

## BELVEDERE PLANTATION GOLF & C. C.

**HAMPSTEAD, NC (From I-40 take exit 210 E. to Rte. 17, N. 4 Mi.)**
**Telephone: (919)270-2703**

Owner:Bridgewater Golf Properties Inc.
Manager/Head Pro: Tom Gibson - PGA
Course Supt.: Ron Taylor
Architect: Russell Burney

18 - R - 6514 - 72

A challenge to players of all levels.
A demanding course with elevated tees and Hybrid 419 fairways.

| | |
|---|---|
| $$ | Resort |
| Golf Pkgs. | Public |
| Power Carts | Lessons |
| Lounge | Snack Bar |
| Meals | Open All Year |

## THE CAPE GOLF & RACQUET CLUB

**WILMINGTON, NC (On Hwy. 421 S., 8 Mi. S. of Wilmington)**
**Telephone: (919)799-3110 Fax: (919)791-2534**

Owner: Thomas Wright
Manager/Head Pro: Margaret Freeman - LPGA
Course Supt.: Randy Edwards
Architect: Gene Hamm

18 - R - 6200 - 72

Features a double green on holes 15 & 17. Bermuda greens and fairways highlighted by twenty four lakes, ponds, and salt water marshes.

| | |
|---|---|
| $$$ | Resort |
| Golf Pkgs. | Public |
| Power Carts | Lessons |
| Lounge | Snack Bar |
| Meals | Open All Year |

## FOX SQUIRREL COUNTRY CLUB

**SOUTHPORT, NC. (6 Mi. N. of Southport, on Hwy. 87)**
**Telephone: (919)845-2625**

Owner/Mgr.: Rick Vigland
Head Pro: Rick Vigland - PGA
Course Supt.: Cale Cooke

**18** - R - 6762 - 72

Beautiful, well maintained Bermuda greens and fairways, sculpted around small freshwater lakes and through towering pines. The course of choice for area residents and tourists.

| | |
|---|---|
| $ | |
| Golf Pkgs. | Public |
| Power Carts | Lessons |
| Lounge | Snack Bar |
| | Open All Year |

## THE GAUNTLET GOLF & COUNTRY CLUB

**SOUTHPORT, NC (20 minutes N. of Myrtle Beach on Hwy. 211)**
**Telephone: (919)253-3008 or: 1-800-247-4806**

Architect: P.B. Dye

18 - R - 6489 - 72

The Gauntlet features all the trademarks that have made Dye courses so famous. Private club service including caddies and club cleaning at daily fee prices.

| | |
|---|---|
| $$$ | |
| Golf Pkgs. | Semi Private |
| Power Carts | Lessons |
| Lounge | Snack Bar |
| Meals | Open All Year |

## LOCKWOOD GOLF LINKS

**HOLDEN BEACH, NC. (Hwy. 17 to Hwy. 130 to Holden Beach, Follow the signs)**
**Telephone: (919)842-5666 US Toll Free: 1-800-443-7891**

Owner/Mgr.: Ernest Hewett
Head Pro: Bobby Blackwell - PGA
Course Supt.: Chuck Brendlen
Architect: Willard C. Byrd

18 - R - 6801 - 72

Located on Lockwood Folly River and Intracoastal Waterway. Tree lined, non-parallel fairways. Bent grass greens.

| | |
|---|---|
| $$$ | Resort |
| Golf Pkgs. | Public |
| Power Carts | Lessons |
| Lounge | Snack Bar |
| Meals | Open All Year |

## OAK ISLAND GOLF & COUNTRY CLUB

**LONG BEACH, NC. (I-95 and I-40 to 17 S. to 133, 1/2 Mi. to Club entrance)**
**Telephone: (919)278-5275**

General Manager: Tom Elder
Head Pro: Tom Elder
Course Supt.: Joe Allegood
Architect: George Cobb

18 - R - 6608 - 72

This championship golf course is located steps away from the Atlantic Ocean. It ambles through live and water oaks. The ocean breeze is a constant factor.

| | |
|---|---|
| $$ | Resort |
| Golf Pkgs. | Public |
| Power Carts | Lessons |
| Lounge | Snack Bar |
| Meals | Open All Year |

## PORTERS NECK PLANTATION & COUNTRY CLUB

**WILMINGTON, NC (On Porters Neck Road. 10 Minutes from Wrightsville Beach)**
**Telephone: (919)686-1177 Sales Info: 1-800-423-5695**

President: John A. Elmore II
Head Pro: Matt Peebles - PGA
Course Supt.: Robert Nance III

18 - R - 6323 - 72

Designed by *Golf Digest's* #1 designer Tom Fazio, this course is already being talked about as one of the best in the Carolina's.

| | |
|---|---|
| $$$ | |
| Golf Pkgs. | Semi Private |
| Power Carts | Lessons |
| Lounge | Snack Bar |
| Meals | Open All Year |

## TEE-TIMES, Inc. GOLF VACATION PACKAGES

With one call to TEE-TIMES central reservation service you can book your entire golf vacation...tee times, lodging, airline tickets and rental car. Choose from 25 coastal courses in Wilmington, North Carolina (minutes north of Myrtle Beach), from world renown Pinehurst area courses, or courses in the Great Smokey Mountains. TEE-TIMES staff are all golfers, have played these North Carolina courses and can help you select exactly the type of facilities you are looking for. ATTRACTIVE PRICES WITH CART FEES AND TAXES INCLUDED, NO COURSE SURCHARGES. Most courses offer ALL DAY GREEN FEES for those who like to play 36 holes / day.

Packages are customized to your specifications with a state-of-the-arts computer system which enables you to shop a variety of hotels & courses in a matter of minutes. Excellent airfares and rental car rates are available with these packages if you are planning to fly. Often below published fares, TEE-TIMES golf airfares require no Saturday stay-over, only 3 day advance purchase, and are refundable if plans change at the last minute. These fares even allow you to fly in and out of two different cities: EXAMPLE: fly into Wilmington, NC for several days of coastal golf, drive to Pinehurst (about 2 hours) for several more days of golf, and then fly home from Pinehurst...NO EXTRA CHARGE! Canadian fares as low as $275 USD round trip from Toronto. Quotes available from all Canadian cities.

**TOPSAIL GREENS**
**GOLF & COUNTRY CLUB**

## TOPSAIL GREENS GOLF & COUNTRY CLUB

**HAMPSTEAD, NC (On US Hwy. #17, 16 Mi. N. of Wilmington)**
**Telephone: (919)270-2883 Fax: (919)270-4921**

Manager: Shanne Murphy
Head Pro: Alex Rachunok
Course Supt.: Dennis Culbreth
Architect: Russel Burney

18 - R - 6010 - 71

Topsail Greens is located just minutes away from Topsail Beach and the Atlantic Ocean.

| | |
|---|---|
| $ | |
| Golf Pkgs. | Public |
| Power Carts | Lessons |
| Lounge | Snack Bar |
| Meals | Open All Year |

DRIVE CAREFULLY
Thank you for visiting ...
NORTH CAROLINA
... Come again soon

GOLF CONNECTIONS

# PENNSYLVANIA

Cross Creek Golf Course

1992/93 DIRECTORY

# Golf Vacations

## PENNSYLVANIA

Pages 129-136

GOLF CONNECTIONS

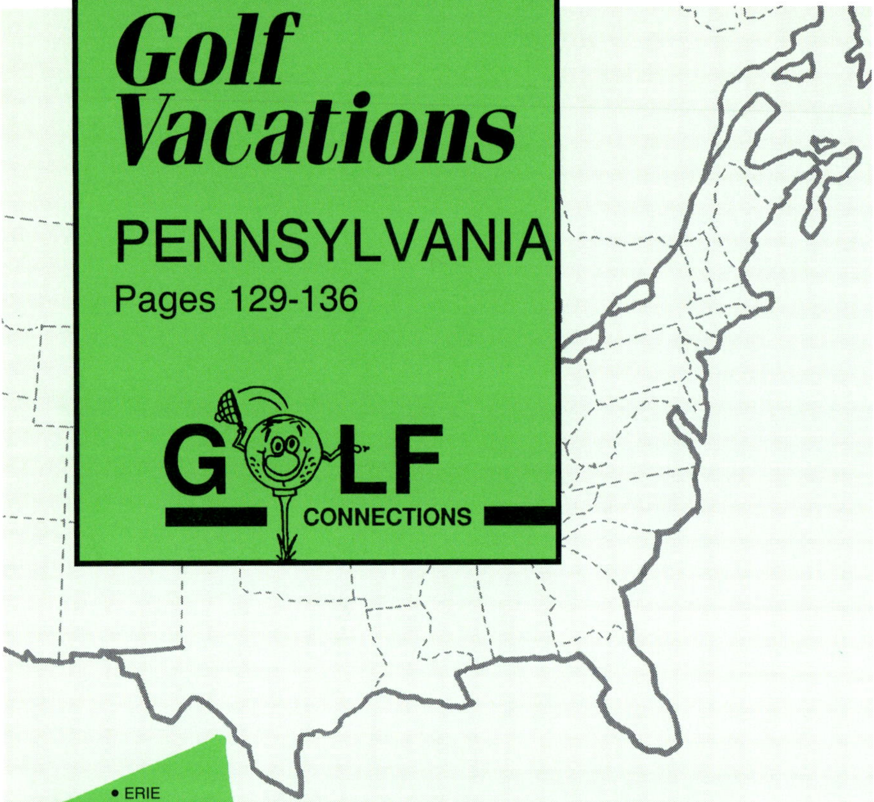

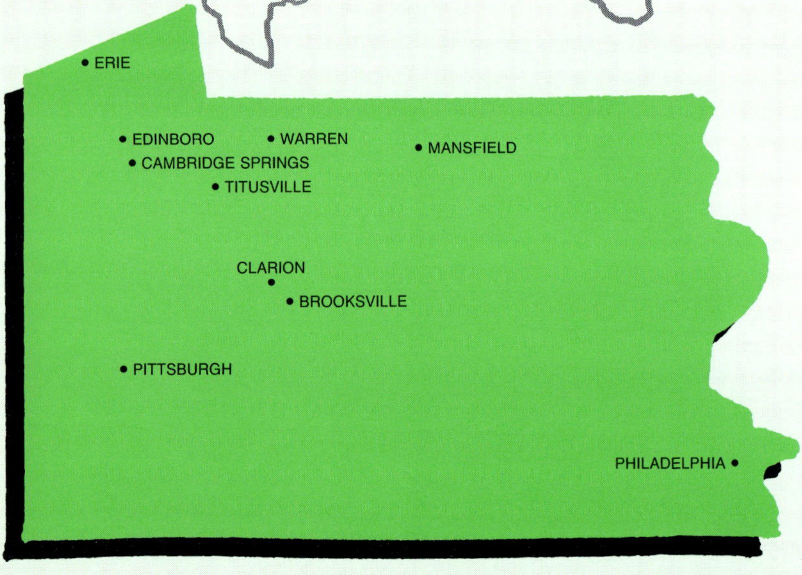


PENNSYLVANIA

## *There's Always A Tee Party At...*

# Cross Creek Resort

Just a 2-1/2 hour drive south of the Canadian / USA border
Titusville, Pennsylvania

*Cross Creek Resort Features:*

- 27 hole Championship Golf Course
- Gourmet Dining
- 94 Luxurious Guest Rooms
- Outdoor Heated Pool
- Tennis Courts
- Crystal Ring Lounge with Revolving Bar
- 19th Hole Lounge
- Amiable Staff and Attentive Service

JOIN US ON THE GREENS THIS SUMMER

**Golf Packages starting at just**

**$199.** PER PERSON (US FUNDS, PLUS 6% TAX)

*All of our Golf Packages Include:*

- Unlimited Golf
- Riding Cart (18 holes per day)
- Buffet Breakfasts
- Buffet Dinners
- Lodging
- AND NO HIDDEN COSTS

Experience all the pleasures of resort golfing without extensive travel and prices.

**CALL US TODAY! (814)827-9611**

4 miles south of Titusville, Pennsylvania on Route 8. One hour south of Interstate 90.

## BLUEBERRY HILL GOLF COURSE

**RUSSELL, PA (On Scandia Rd., follow signs from Warren, PA)**
**Telephone: (814)757-8620  Lodge: (814)757-8690**

Manager: Charles Irvin
Head Pro: Jill Jerauld
Course Supt.: Don Holmberg
Architect: Ferdinand Garbin

18 - R - 6428 - 72

Additional 9 Holes under construction.
Remodelled clubhouse available to cater banquets and parties up to 200. Lodge facilities available as well as over 60 building lots.

| | |
|---|---|
| $ | |
| Golf Pkgs. | Public |
| Power Carts | Lessons |
| Lounge | Snack Bar |
| Meals | |

cable hollow golf

## CABLE HOLLOW GOLF CLUB

**RUSSELL, PA (Between Jamestown & Warren)**
**Office: (814)757-9977  Pro Shop: (814)757-4765**

Owners: John & Marge Bortz
Clubhouse Manager: John Bortz, Jr.
Course Supt.: David Bortz

18 - R - 5832 - 71

Cable Hollow has been operated by the Bortz family since 1972. For 20 years they have created new and challenging layouts with the addition of bunkers, sand traps and landscape changes. Original aerial photos are in the pro shop.

| | |
|---|---|
| $ | |
| Golf Pkgs. | Public |
| Power Carts | |
| Lounge | Snack Bar |
| Meals | |

## CULBERTSON HILLS GOLF CLUB

**EDINBORO, PA (2 Mi. E. of I-19, from exit #38)**
**Telephone: (814)734-5650  Fax: (814)734-1332**
**Canadian Toll Free: 1-800-227-8448**

Manager: Bob Orr, Sr.
Head Pro: Bob Orr, Jr.
Course Supt.: Janet Gibas

18 - R - 6444 - 72

Accommodations available on site at the EDINBORO INN (See page 133).

| | |
|---|---|
| $ | Resort |
| Golf Pkgs. | Public |
| Power Carts | Lessons |
| Lounge | Snack Bar |
| Meals | |

## COREY CREEK GOLF CLUB

**MANSFIELD, PA**
**Telephone: (717)662-3520**

Head Pro: Art Connelly
Course Supt.: Art Connelly
Architects: Herb Peterson/Jack Marsh

18 - R - 6164 - 72

| | |
|---|---|
| $ | |
| Golf Pkgs. | Public |
| Power Carts | Lessons |
| Lounge | Snack Bar |
| Meals | |

An 18 hole course set in the Appalachian Mountains of northern Pennsylvania. It features quick, undulating greens with creeks and lakes on 12 holes.

## RIVERSIDE GOLF COURSE

**CAMBRIDGE SPRINGS, PA**
**Telephone: (814)398-4692**

Owner: John Britton
General Manager: Anthony Ferraro
Head Pro: Steve Carney
Course Supt.: Dick Ball

18 - R - 6150 - 70
Rating: Men's - 69.2, Ladies' - 70.2

| | |
|---|---|
| $ | |
| | Public |
| Power Carts | Lessons |
| Lounge | Snack Bar |
| | |

**PAR 5. SUNDAY STRETCH**

GOLF

Sunday (after 1 p.m.), Monday & Tuesday

Two Nights Lodging

1 Dinner for 1 — 1 Breakfast for 1

**$139.00**

**Edinboro Inn Resort**
**& Conference Center**

- **Culbertson Hills Golf Club**
- **Riverside Golf Course**

**814-734-5650**

**For Reservations Only Call:**

Continental USA ..................... 1-800-352-3182
Canada ............................ 1-800-227-8448

Located just 20 minutes
South of Erie, Pennsylvania
on I-79, Exit 38

Per person, double occupancy. Based on US. Funds.
Other Golf Packages Available, Call for more information.

DAYS INN

Rt. 68 & I-80
CLARION, PA 16214

Rt. 36 & I-80
BROOKVILLE, PA 15825

## GETAWAY GOLF PACKAGES:

from **$49.00** (per person)
(minimum double occ.)

PACKAGE INCLUDES:

- Complimentary Welcome Cocktail
- One Nights Lodging
- One Full American Breakfast
- 10% Discount on Lunch or Dinner in our Dining Room
- 18 Holes Championship Golf
- Shared Cart Rental

## PLAY THESE FINE COURSES:

***Mayfield Golf Club***
*One of Western Pennsylvania's premier championship courses, Mayfield's 18 holes and 6990 yards of challenge are nestled in the heart of the Magic Forest. Long, tree-lined fairways, water hazards and bunkers will test every club in your bag.*

***Hi-Level Golf Club***
*This executive course is easy to walk and perfect for tuning up your game. Take advantage of the 5 hole practice course before enjoying 18 holes of fun filled golf.*

***Foxburg Country Club***
*Enjoy two rounds of golf on this scenic 9 hole course, the oldest in continuous play in the U.S. View the wild waters of the upper Allegheny River and be ready to spend time in the quaint Log Clubhouse which is the present home of the American Golf Hall of Fame.*

***Pinecrest Country Club***
*Minutes from either Days Inn is the Pinecrest Country Club. Slick greens and winding tree-lined fairways are but two of the challenges that await you on this 18 hole course.*

FOR MORE INFORMATION & RESERVATIONS CALL:

**CLARION**
**(814) 226-8689**

**BROOKVILLE**
**(814) 849-2000**

Holiday Inn

## WARREN, PA

**Holiday Inn of Warren**, nestled in the mountains of the Allegheny National Forest invites you to participate in our area's many summer attractions.

**Golf Courses** all within 30 minutes of your hotel. Play a different course every day, or play your favorite course until your heart's content at the following courses:

* Blueberry Hill
* Cable Hollow
* Pine Acres
* Jackson Valley

## GOLF PACKAGE FOR TWO*

**$125.00** per person

(Based on double occupancy / tax and gratuity included)

• Two nights lodging - 2:00 PM Check Out • A complimentary cocktail • One breakfast - Morning of your choice • One dinner - night of your choice • One round of golf for two with shared cart • Golf widow package available • Non-meal package also available

**Hotel Amenities:** • Indoor pool and sauna • Tootsie's Nightclub with entertainment, DJ, and dancing • Fine Dining restaurant • Plenty of free parking • Exercise and game room • Banquet facilities for large groups • Beautiful garden atrium • Box lunches available

**Area Attractions:** • Blair Clothing Outlet, largest clothing and mail order outlet in USA • Kinzua Dam and Reservoir • Chapman State Park • Many antique dealers in the area • Many unusual shops and boutiques • Library Theatre Summer Playhouse

FOR RESERVATIONS CONTACT

HOLIDAY INN WARREN

210 LUDLOW STREET, WARREN, PA 16365

**(814)726-3000 • 800-H-INN-814**

DRIVE CAREFULLY
Thank you for visiting ...
PENNSYLVANIA
... Come again soon

GOLF CONNECTIONS

# SOUTH CAROLINA

Pages 137-168

Palmetto Dunes Resort

1992/93 DIRECTORY

# *Golf Vacations*

## SOUTH CAROLINA

Pages 137-168

GOLF CONNECTIONS

CN
1786
1986

## CHARLESTON NATIONAL COUNTRY CLUB

**MT. PLEASANT, SC (On Hwy. 17 N., across from the East Cooper Airport)**
**Office: (803)884-7705 Pro Shop: (803)884-7799**

Manager: Philip Perry
Head Pro: Larry Young
Course Supt.: Gayle Franklin
Architect: Rees Jones

18 - R - 6532 - 72

Set in a wildlife reserve this course has over a mile of wooden bridges and over 150 sand traps.

| | |
|---|---|
| $$$ | |
| Golf Pkgs. | Public |
| Power Carts | Lessons |
| | Snack Bar |
| | Open All Year |

CROWFIELD
GOLF & COUNTRY CLUB

## CROWFIELD GOLF & COUNTRY CLUB

**GOOSE CREEK, SC (On Hamlet Circle, off College Park Rd., exit 203 off Hwy. 26)**
**Telephone: (803)764-4618 Fax: (803)764-4534**

Owners: Kemper Sports Management
Head Pro: Marty Mikesell - PGA
Course Supt.: Scot Ferguson
Architect: Bob Spence

18 - R - 6471 - 72

| | |
|---|---|
| $ | |
| Golf Pkgs. | Public |
| Power Carts | Lessons |
| Lounge | Snack Bar |
| Meals | Open All Year |

## HERITAGE GOLF CLUB

**PAWLEY'S ISLAND, SC (S. on Hwy. 17, 1Mi. past stop light. Entrance on right)**
**Telephone: (803)626-5121**

Head Pro: Dave Rastello

18 - R - 7100 - 71
Rating: Men's - 76.5, Ladies' - 71

| | |
|---|---|
| $$$ | Resort |
| Golf Pkgs. | Public |
| Power Carts | Lessons |
| Lounge | Snack Bar |
| Meals | Open All Year |

## ISLAND GREEN GOLF & COUNTRY CLUB

**SURFSIDE BEACH, SC (Rte. 707, between Socastee & Murrells Inlet)**
**Telephone: (803)650-2186**

Head Pro: Richard Roberge - PGA

27 Holes

This 27 hole course is built upon gently rolling terrain and is accented with an abundance of azaleas and dogwoods. Several holes include island and peninsula greens. Superbly conditioned fairways and lush Burmuda greens make this course a favorite. Friendly atmosphere.

| | |
|---|---|
| $$$ | Resort |
| Golf Pkgs. | |
| Power Carts | Lessons |
| Lounge | Snack Bar |
| Meals | Open All Year |

## SHADOWMOSS PLANTATION GOLF COURSE

**CHARLESTON, SC (3 1/2 Mi. from Ashley River Rd. exit, off 526 to Savanna)**
**Telephone: (803)556-8251 Toll Free: 1-800-338-4971**

Manager: Jeannie Simmons
Head Pro: Victor Grubbs - PGA
Course Supt.: Steve Long

18 - R - 6399 - 72

A challenging layout with lush fairways carved through a forest of old oaks & hickorys, amidst a mosaic of ponds and streams.

| | |
|---|---|
| $$ | |
| Golf Pkgs. | Public |
| Power Carts | Lessons |
| Lounge | Snack Bar |
| | Open All Year |

# MYRTLE BEACH HILTON

OCEANFRONT GOLF RESORT

*Featuring Arcadian Shores Golf Club*

## A GREAT PLACE TO STAY

*THE MYRTLE BEACH HILTON is a great place to stay when in Myrtle Beach, whether you are on a golf holiday, a business trip, or just taking in a few days of R & R.*

*GOLF CONNECTIONS had the opportunity to stay at the HILTON last fall and we thoroughly enjoyed our two day visit. The staff was pleasant and the food, service and accommodations, were what we expected from the HILTON.*

*This four star/four diamond hotel has 392 newly decorated rooms, all of them overlooking the ocean and white, sandy beach. Four tennis courts and an oceanside heated swimming pool with deck are provided for hotel guests and, in season, the "Poolside Terrace" restaurant and "Wet Whistle" poolside bar are open for extra convenience.*

*The "Arcadian Gardens" restaurant will get your day started with a healthy breakfast (other meals are also served there) and for a romantic, evening gourmet meal "Alfredo's" is the place to be.*

## GOLF PACKAGES AVAILABLE

*The MYRTLE BEACH HILTON offers attractive golf packages. Their daily rate ranges from $46.00 per person (off season) to $83.00 per person (prime time) based on double occupancy.*

*This includes oceanview accommodations, breakfast, one green fee per night's stay (choose from over 60 area courses), free transportation to Acadian Shores Golf Club, meal gratuities, and taxes.*

*Other golf packages are available (3 days or 6 days) and dinner at "Alfredo's" can be included.*

For more information contact:

MYRTLE BEACH HILTON
Myrtle Beach, SC 29572-5304
**Toll Free: 1-800-248-9228**

# ACADIAN SHORES GOLF CLUB

**MYRTLE BEACH (701 Hilton Road)**

Telephone: (803)449-5217

Head Pro: Aubrey Apple - PGA
Course Supt: Jay Johnson
Architect: Rees Jones

18 - R - 6468 - 72    Rating: Men's - 71.1, Ladies' - 69.9
Slope: Men's - 131, Ladies' - 117

| | |
|---|---|
| $$ | Resort |
| Golf Pkgs. | Public |
| Power Carts | Lessons |
| Lounge | Snack Bar |
| Meals | Open All Year |

This course is well-manicured and interesting to play. Water comes into play on 8 holes. Four sets of tee blocks allow for a real choice of challenge.

## PAWLEYS PLANTATION GOLF & COUNTRY CLUB

**PAWLEYS ISLAND, SC (On Highway 17)**
**Villas Rentals: 1-800-367-9959** **Golf School: 1-800-624-4653**

Owner/Manager: Les Morris
Head Pro: Ronnie Cauthen
Course Supt.: Bill Ashley
Architect: Jack Nicklaus

18 - R - 7026 - 72

A Jack Nicklaus signature golf course. Need we say more?

| | |
|---|---|
| $$$ | Resort |
| Golf Pkgs. | |
| Power Carts | Lessons |
| Lounge | Snack Bar |
| Meals | Open All Year |

## SEABROOK ISLAND RESORT

**SEABROOK ISLAND, SC (Off Hwy. 17 South)**

**Telephone: (803)768-1000 Fax: (803)768-4922**

Manager: Tom Halsey
Head Pro: Bruce Gerlander
Architects: Robert Trent Jones / Willard Byrd

36 holes: 18 - R - 6880 - 72
18 - R - 6549 - 72

These two championship courses are located in Seabrook Island Resort, a private 2200 acre island. Only club members and rental guests are permitted access to these beautiful facilities.

| | |
|---|---|
| $$$ | Resort |
| Golf Pkgs. | |
| Power Carts | Lessons |
| Lounge | Snack Bar |
| Meals | Open All Year |

## WILD DUNES RESORT

**CHARLESTON, SC (On the Isle of Palms, off Hwy. 703, from Hwy. 17)**
**Telephone: (803)886-6000 Fax: (803)886-2916**

Manager: Jeff Akers
Head Pro: Terry Florence
Course Supt.: Mike Fabrizio
Architect: Tom Fazio

36 holes: Links Course - 18 - R - 6722 - 72
Harbour Course - 18 - R - 6466 - 70

| | |
|---|---|
| $$$ | Resort |
| Golf Pkgs. | Semi-Private |
| Power Carts | Lessons |
| Lounge | Snack Bar |
| Meals | Open All Year |

## THE GOLF PROFESSIONALS CLUB

**BEAUFORT, SC (At Lady's Island, off Rte. 802 E. from Hilton Head Island)**
**Telephone: (803)522-9700** **Pro Shop: (803)524-3635**

Director of Golf: Dick Tremblay

Course Record: 64 - Joe Staffieri
Champions Course: 18 - R - 6650 - 72
Players Course: 18 - R - 5800 - 72

Stretching out to 7150 yards from the tournament tees, the Champions Course was designed to attract PGA and LPGA Professionals in their off season. Open to amateur play both courses are less demanding from the white tees.

| | |
|---|---|
| $$ | |
| Golf Pkgs. | Public |
| Power Carts | Lessons |
| Lounge | Snack Bar |
| Meals | Open All Year |

## OLD SOUTH GOLF LINKS

**HILTON HEAD, SC (On Hwy. 278, across from Moss Creek Plantation)**
**Telephone: (803)785-5353**

Manager: David W. Staley
Head Pro: Brady R. Boyd
Course Supt.: Scott Adams
Architect: Clyde Johnston

18 - R - 6354 - 72

This course has 7 holes on the marsh overlooking the Intracoastal Waterway and includes an island green.

| | |
|---|---|
| $$$ | Resort |
| Golf Pkgs. | Public |
| Power Carts | Lessons |
| Lounge | Snack Bar |
| Meals | Open All Year |

Opened in 1991 and already one of the top rated courses in the low country area, OLD SOUTH GOLF LINKS is located at the foot of the bridge to Hilton Head Island. It's imaginative design is the concept of Clyde Johnston, creator of two of *Golf Digest's* top rated new courses in the last five years.

Playing 6,774 yards from the back tees, this exciting par-72 course is located along the Intracoastal Waterway, with seven of its eighteen holes overlooking the sound.

*"Old South Golf Links was designed not only to provide an enjoyable yet challenging golf game, but also to preserve the natural beauty of the land. I felt this was an opportunity to allow the golfer to experience up close the uniqueness of the site, its natural amenities and spectacular view.*

*The variety of settings from oak forests to open pasture to tidal salt marsh provided an opportunity to vary the design elements and strategy of play. Old South will soon become one of the classic course in the south."*
- Clyde B. Johnston

OLD SOUTH GOLF LINKS is open to the public seven days a week and features a full line pro shop to meet all of your golfing needs.

# PALMETTO DUNES RESORT

HILTON HEAD ISLAND, S.C.

## " FROM TEE TO SHINING SEA"

PALMETTO DUNES is one of Hilton Head's finest vacation resorts. A unique combination of luxurious one to four bedroom villas located on the ocean, harbour and fairways; clean, beautiful beach, world class golf and tennis facilities.

Three 18 hole championship golf courses, each named after its world-renowned designer have been built on this 2000 acre resort Robert Trent Jones, George Fazio and Arthur Hills. (See listings following).

## GOLF PACKAGES

Golf Packages are available year round and include fully-furnished villa, 18 holes of golf per day, preferred starting times, limited housekeeping services and free daily tennis at the 25 court Palmetto Dunes Tennis Center.

The resort is perfect for the family with bikes, pools, shopping, dining, summer children's program and much more. For more information contact:

PALMETTO DUNES RESORT
P.O. Box 5606, Hilton Head Island SC 29938
**1-800-845-6130** (US & Canada)

## GEORGE FAZIO COURSE

**HILTON HEAD ISLAND, SC (Palmetto Dunes Resort)**
**Telephone: (803)785-1130**

Director of Golf: Chip Pellerin
Head Pro: Bill Layman
Course Supt.: John Betts
Architect: George Fazio

| | |
|---|---|
| $$$ | Resort |
| Golf Pkgs. | Public |
| Power Carts | Lessons |
| Lounge | Snack Bar |
| Meals | Open All Year |

18 - R - 6239 - 70 Rating: Men's - 71.2, Ladies' - 69.2

This course has appeared on GOLF DIGEST'S list of America's 100 best. With only two par 5's, the heart of the course lies in a series of long par 4's.

## ARTHUR HILLS COURSE

**HILTON HEAD ISLAND, SC (Palmetto Dunes Resort)**
**Telephone: (803)785-1140**

Director of Golf: Chip Pellerin
Head Pro: Bob Faulkner
Course Supt.: John Betts
Architect: Arthur Hills

18 - R - 6122 - 72 Rating: Men's - 69.3, Ladies' - 68.2

Dunes, thick stands of Palmettos, a violently rolling layout with dramatic elevation changes. One of the most distinctive in the area. Off balance lies, ocean breezes and lagoons require ball control and course management.

| | |
|---|---|
| $$$ | Resort |
| Golf Pkgs. | Public |
| Power Carts | Lessons |
| Lounge | Snack Bar |
| Meals | Open All Year |

## ROBERT TRENT JONES COURSE

**HILTON HEAD ISLAND, SC (Palmetto Dunes Resort)**
**Telephone: (803)785-1138**

Director of Golf: Chip Pellerin
Head Pro: Clark Sinclair
Course Supt.: John Betts
Architect: Robert Trent Jones

18 - R - 6148 - 72 Rating: Men's - 69.3, Ladies' - 70.7

A unique winding lagoon system comes into play on 11 of the 18 holes. The par 5, 10th. hole provides a breathtaking view of the Atlantic Ocean.

| | |
|---|---|
| $$$ | Resort |
| Golf Pkgs. | Public |
| Power Carts | Lessons |
| Lounge | Snack Bar |
| Meals | Open All Year |



## PALMETTO HALL PLANTATION

**HILTON HEAD ISLAND, SC**
**Telephone: (803)689-4100**

Director of Golf: Chip Pellerin
Course Supt.: Tom Metzger
Architect: Arthur Hills

18 - R - 6257 - 72 Rating: Men's - 70.5, Ladies - 68.9

Subtle contouring, distinctive layout and a touch of Arthur Hills genius. Fairways wind through deep thickets of oak and pine and the course is punctuated with sparkling lakes. A challenging, scenic joy.

| | |
|---|---|
| $$$ | Resort |
| Golf Pkgs. | Public |
| Power Carts | Lessons |
| Lounge | Snack Bar |
| Meals | Open All Year |

HiltonHead National

A **GARY PLAYER** SIGNATURE GOLF COURSE

## HILTON HEAD NATIONAL

**HILTON HEAD ISLAND, SC**

**Telephone: (803)842-5900 Fax: (803)837-5502**

Director of Golf: Bob Mendenhall
Course Supts.: Mike Cam/Blake Caryle
Architect: Gary Player

18 - R - 6260 - 72 Rating: Men's - 70.6
Course Record: 64 - Jim Thorpe

This course offers a visual feast and a varied set of challenges set naturally into the landscape in the Scottish tradition. Strategy is required more often than strength which sums up Gary Player's design philosophy.

| | |
|---|---|
| $$$ | |
| | Public |
| Power Carts | Lessons |
| Lounge | Snack Bar |
| Meals | Open All Year |

## SHIPYARD GOLF & RACQUET CLUB

### HILTON HEAD ISLAND, SC

**Telephone: (803)686-8802**

Director of Golf: Peter Rouillard
Teaching Pro: Ron Cerrudo
Course Supt.: James Norby
Architects: George Cobb/Willard Byrd

3 x 9 holes - R - 6167 - 72 Rating: Men's - 69.7, Ladies' - 70.5
Accurate tee shots and well thought approaches are required. Undulating greens are large and well bunkered.

| | |
|---|---|
| $$$ | Resort |
| Golf Pkgs. | Public |
| Power Carts | Lessons |
| Lounge | Snack Bar |
| Meals | Open All Year |

ROSE HILL
COUNTRY CLUB

## ROSE HILL COUNTRY CLUB

**BLUFFTON, SC (Hwy. 278, 6 miles from Hilton Head Island)**
**Telephone: (803)757-2160**

Manager: John A. Capes - CHA - VP Club Operations
Director of Golf: Brian Quigley - PGA
Course Supt.: Rob Ouellette
Architect: Gene Hamm

27 holes: 18 - R - 6276 - 18
Rose Hill Country Club offers 27 holes of championship golf with excellent practice facilities and a delightful low country clubhouse with dining room and pro shop.

| | |
|---|---|
| $$ | |
| Golf Pkgs. | Public |
| Power Carts | Lessons |
| Lounge | Snack Bar |
| Meals | Open All Year |

## WEXFORD PLANTATION

**HILTON HEAD ISLAND, SC**
**Telephone: (803)686-8812**

Manager: George Boyland
Head Pro: Keith Goodaker
Architect: Willard Byrd

18 Holes Regulation

DRIVE CAREFULLY
Thank you for visiting . . .
HILTON HEAD AREA
. . . Come again soon

Right off I-95 at Exit 98 (Highway 6) just across the bridge over Lake Marion (if you are travelling south) is SANTEE, SC

Already well known for hunting and fishing opportunities, more and more golfers are discovering that SANTEE offers some of the finest golf courses to be found in the south / eastern states.

Excellent accommodations for one, two, or two hundred are available and most of the motel / hotels offer golf packages at exceptionally attractive rates.

***TRY IT ONCE . . . YOU'LL COME BACK FOR MORE !!!***

## LAKE MARION GOLF COURSE

**SANTEE, SC. ( Located 200 yds. E. of exit 98, off I-95, 12 Mi. N. of I-26)**
**Telephone: (803)854-2554** **Toll Free: 1-800-344-6534**
**Fax:(803)854-2029**

Dir. of Golf: Carroll Pifer
Course Supt.: John Livingston

18 - R - 6616 - 72

This course offers gently rolling hills and wide fairways lined with native foliage. Challenging to the low handicapper, it also provides an enjoyable round for the beginner. Very friendly, professional service.

| | |
|---|---|
| $$ | Resort |
| Golf Pkgs. | Public |
| Power Carts | Lessons |
| | Snack Bar |
| | Open All Year |

## SANTEE COOPER COUNTRY CLUB

**SANTEE, SC. ( Located 200 yds. E. of exit 98, off I-95, 12 Mi. N. of I-26)**
**Resort Office: (803)854-2233** **Pro Shop: (803)854-2467**
**Fax: (803)854-2029**

Dir. of Golf: Carroll Pifer

18 - R - 6512 - 72

This country club is located within Santee-Cooper Resort where homes and homesites adjoin the fairways, greens or water of Lake Marion. The course provides a wide variety of challenges to golfers of every level.

GOLF 1992

Quality Inn

# Clark's Motel & restaurant

P.O. Box 26 • I-95 @ SC Hwy 6
Santee, South Carolina 29142
Telephone: 1-803-845-2141
In Canada Toll Free: 1-800-345-7888

*We're conveniently located off I-95 in Santee, South Carolina with easy access from all major southern routes (I-26, I-95, I20 & I-77)*

*Our location, great rates, and fabulous accommodations make Quality Inn Clark's & Santee National Golf Club a winning combination in Santee Cooper Country!*
*Call or write today for further details!*

P.O. Drawer 190 • SC Hwy 6 West
Santee, South Carolina
**1-803-854-3531**

SANTEE NATIONAL golf club

# SANTEE COOPER COUNTRY

*Great Golf - Great People and . . . Jakes!!!*

May / 90 GOLF CONNECTIONS accepted an invitation from the Santee Cooper Counties Promotion Commission to participate in a three day "Test Drive" of SANTEE's golf courses.

We thoroughly enjoyed our stay at Clark's Quality Inn, a fine Inn with restaurant adjacent, and we managed to play a number of the golf courses (all excellent).

Two main impressions were left with us - what great value the folks at SANTEE were offering golfers in their packages and what congenial hospitality and service awaits that golfer upon arrival.

Carroll Pifer, Director of Golf for Santee Cooper Resort and the Lake Marion Golf Club is perhaps the one most responsible for the increase in packaged golf play in Santee. As an example . . .

Last fall he sent us a fax to advise us of his latest, off-season golf package special . . . $25.00 for accommodations, unlimited golf with cart (per person/day) - at the bottom of the fax was added "You can't live at home this cheaply !!" He was right and the promotion scored well.

Bob Finney is another reason why golfers will now spend some quality time at SANTEE.

While General Manager of Clark's Quality Inn, Bob and his lovely wife Donna travelled extensively (in Canada and US), participating in promotional events and shows, manning booths, encouraging golfers to visit SANTEE.

To GOLF CONNECTIONS, Bob and Donna, with their happy, unpretentious nature, and down-home charm epitomized what we believed SANTEE to be all about. They are just great to be with.

Last September we paid a return visit to SANTEE just in time for lunch. We wanted to check out "Jakes" - the new place for Steaks & Ribs in Santee.

It was filled with people, savouring plentiful servings of "Jakes" finest . . . and there was Bob, flipping steaks and ribs over the charcoal, smiling, being everywhere at once, and still selling SANTEE.

When we asked him how come the name "Jakes" and not "Bob's" or "Donna's" he just pointed to the huge, framed photograph of a beautiful, smiling two year old, hung high over the hearth . . . "That's my grandson. His name is Jake. . .and he owns this place!"

So this one's for you JAKE !!!

**Jakes STEAKS & RIBS**

***What your taste buds have been waiting for!***

Located I-95 at Exit 98 on Hwy. 6 East • Santee, SC (803)854-3999

PINE FOREST Country Club

## PINE FOREST COUNTRY CLUB

**SUMMERVILLE, SC (On Central Ave., from 17A off exit #199 from I-26)**
**Telephone: (803)851-1193 Fax: (803)851-2857**

Owner: Kemper Sports Management
Head Pro: Shane Cleveland
Course Supt.: Tom Cannon
Architect: Ken Killian

18 - R - 6256 - 72

This course is nestled amongst pines and pristine lakes, it is one of the best new courses in the historic Low Country.

| | |
|---|---|
| $$$ | Resort |
| Golf Pkgs. | Public |
| Power Carts | Lessons |
| Lounge | Snack Bar |
| Meals | Open All Year |

# SUMTER, SOUTH CAROLINA
## A "TEE-RIFIC" NEW GOLF MECCA

How many golfers in Canada had ever heard of Sumter, South Carolina before 1987? Probably nobody.

That is why in 1987, Jule Eldridge, an enterprising Hotel owner in Sumter, S.C. met with seven local golf course owners and convinced them to join up with his Hotel to form a *Golf Package.* An appropriate name was adopted . . . **TEE-RIFIC GOLF.**

The results have been astonishing. In 1990, over 12,000 **TEE-RIFIC GOLF** rounds were played by individuals from all over the United States and Canada and that record was exceeded in 1991.

GOLF CONNECTIONS had an opportunity to visit with Jule Eldridge in Sumter in August 1991 and we were most impressed with this man, his concept, his kindness and his enthusiasm. (Space does not allow us to comment on his remarkable golf swing).

"Golf in 1992 looks even stronger," says Eldridge, adding "Over half of our golfers are either repeat customers or have learned about us from the recommendation of a friend. We hear that over-and-over whenever our telephone rings".

Today, thirty-three (33) Sumter area golf courses (private, public and semi-private) participate in **TEE-RIFIC GOLF** which is headquartered at the RAMADA INN of SUMTER (formerly The Park Inn Hotel). Thirty of them are listed on the following page and their location is pinpointed on the map pages provided in this section.

With such a number of courses involved, the golf packages are tailored to accommodate every kind of golfer. Just tell them what you want in a golf course and they will match you up with the ones that interest you. If you wish you can play 36 holes every day and the only extra charge for the "second 18" is a nominal cart fee.

A multi- page magazine about **TEE-RIFIC GOLF** is printed semi-annually and is available FREE for the asking.

TEE-RIFIC GOLF is indeed one of the most outstanding golf packages anywhere and the reasonable prices are exceeded only by the hospitality, history, and charm of the Sumter community.

**FOR MORE INFORMATION AND RESERVATIONS**
**CALL TOLL FREE: 1-800-457-6884**

## HERE IS YOUR "TEE-RIFIC" HOST IN SUMTER S.C.

JULE ELDRIDGE
Hotelier • Realtor • Founder

### HERE ARE THE "TEE-RIFIC" GOLF COURSES

(See course locations on maps - following pages)

1. Beech Creek Plantation
2. Pineland Plantation
3. Lakewood Links
4. Pocalla Springs
5. Crystal Lakes G.C.
6. Carolina Lakes G.C.
7. Clarendon Golf & C.C.
8. Foxboro Golf Course
9. Santee National C.C.
10. Lake Marion G.C.
11. Santee-Cooper C.C.
12. Calhoun C.C.
13. Hillcrest Golf & Tennis C.
14. Paw Paw G.C.
15. Dogwood Hills G.C.
16. Lake City C.C.
17. Wellman C.C.
18. Dusty Hills C.C.
19. Bishopville C.C.
20. Fox Creek G.C.
21. The Country Club of SC
22. Tifton G.C.
23. Sandy point G.C.
24. Sedgewood C.C.
25. Northwoods G.C.
26. Oak Hills G.C.
27. Charwood C.C.
28. Hidden Valley G.C.
29. Coldstream C.C.
30. Timberlake G.C.

. . . and recent additions

So many golfers have returned for a third, fourth, or fifth annual pilgrimage to Sumter that Jule Eldridge now offers a specialized Golf Real Estate Service. If you are thinking of investing for your retirement in a Golf Course lot, the Sumter area has lots priced as low as $13,500. ($US price in 1991). Find out more. Ask for a copy of MOVIN' SOUTH, Carolina's Relocation and Retirement Report.

**ELDRIDGE REALTY COMPANY**
P.O. Box 520 • Sumter, SC 29151
**1-800-277-3847 (US)**
Tel: (803) 775-1266 Fax: (803) 775-1267

# RAMADA® INN

226 N. WASHINGTON ST., SUMTER, SC 29151

- 125 Upscale Hotel Rooms and Suites
- King-Sized Beds - with Sofas
- Non-Smoking and Adjoining Rooms
- Children under 18, Free in Room with Parent
- Cable Color TV • Movie Channels
- Direct Dial Phones - Free Local Calls
- Same-Day Laundry & Dry Cleaning Services
- Restaurant • Lounge
- Meeting Rooms • Teleconferencing • Wide-Screen TV
- Landscaped Grounds • On-Premise Putting Green
- Handicap Facilities - Elevator • Ample Free Parking
- All Major Credit Cards Honored

## •Dining & Meeting Facilities

Delicious Meals Served Daily in our Restaurant

Refreshing Drinks and Tasty Snacks in *"Mulligans"* Lounge

## •Relaxation & Entertainment

- Swimming Pool
- Convenient Shopping
- Unique Antique Row
- Historical Tours
- Hunting & Fishing
- Swan Lake Iris Gardens
- Putting Green
- Academy Golf School

**FOR MORE INFORMATION AND RESERVATIONS**
**CALL TOLL FREE: 1-800-457-6884**

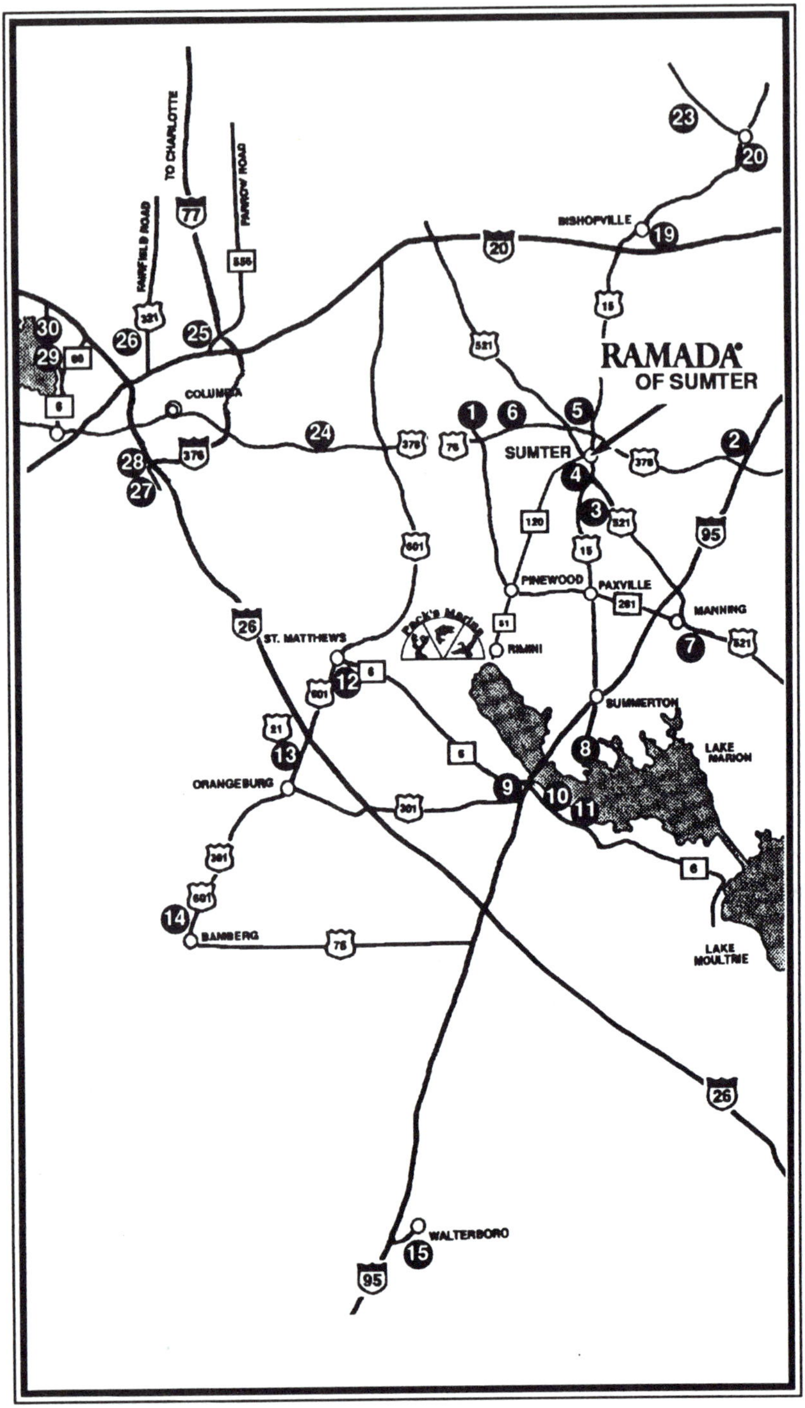
TO CHARLOTTE
FAIRFIELD ROAD
FARROW ROAD
BISHOPVILLE
RAMADA® OF SUMTER
COLUMBIA
SUMTER
PINEWOOD
PAXVILLE
MANNING
ST. MATTHEWS
Pack's Marina
RIMINI
SUMMERTON
LAKE MARION
ORANGEBURG
BAMBERG
LAKE MOULTRIE
WALTERBORO

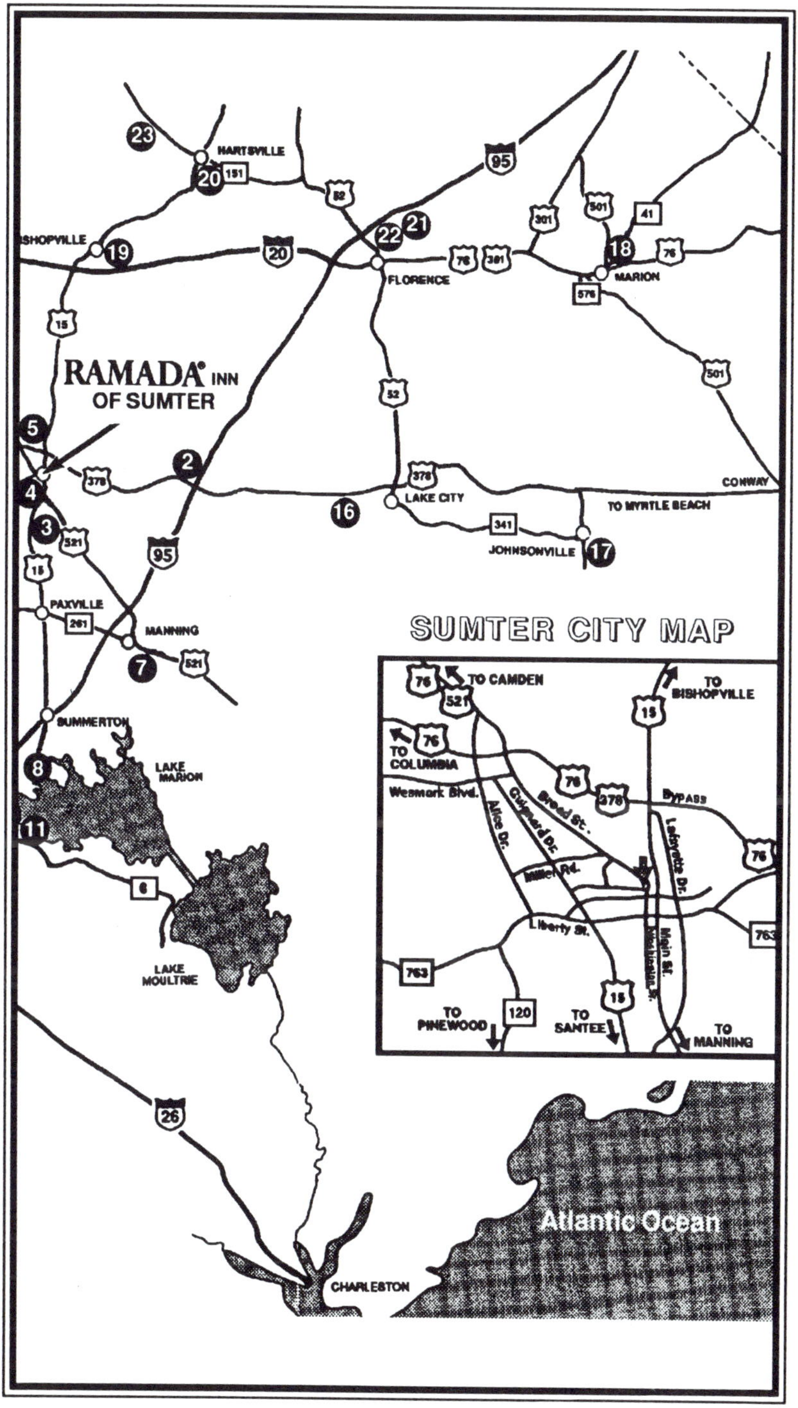

HARTSVILLE
BISHOPVILLE
FLORENCE
MARION
RAMADA® INN
OF SUMTER
CONWAY
LAKE CITY
TO MYRTLE BEACH
JOHNSONVILLE
PAXVILLE
MANNING
SUMMERTON
LAKE MARION
LAKE MOULTRIE
SUMTER CITY MAP
TO CAMDEN
TO BISHOPVILLE
TO COLUMBIA
Wesmark Blvd.
Alice Dr.
Guignard Dr.
Broad St.
Bypass
Lafayette Dr.
Miller Rd.
Liberty St.
Main St.
Washington St.
TO PINEWOOD
TO SANTEE
TO MANNING
Atlantic Ocean
CHARLESTON

## BEECH CREEK GOLF CLUB

**SUMTER, SC (On Sam Gillespie Rd.)**
**Telephone: (803)499-4653**

Head Pro: E.B. Bell
Course Supt.: E.B. Bell
Architect: James Goodson

18 - R - 5978 - 72

This course features 4 of the best finishing holes in the state.
Water comes into play on 6 of the 18 holes.
See pages 159-161 for "Tee-riffic" golf package reservation details.

| | |
|---|---|
| $ | |
| Golf Pkgs. | Public |
| Power Carts | Lessons |
| Lounge | Snack Bar |
| | Open All Year |

## BISHOPVILLE COUNTRY CLUB

**BISHOPVILLE, SC (On Hwy. 15 S., 2 miles S. of Interstate 20)**
**Telephone: (803)428-3675**

Proprietor: William Watkins

18 - R - 5650 - 72

This course has Bermuda greens and fairways.
See pages 159-161 for "Tee-rific" Golf Package reservation details.

| | |
|---|---|
| $ | |
| Golf Pkgs. | Public |
| Power Carts | Lessons |
| Lounge | Snack Bar |
| | Open All Year |

## HILLCREST GOLF COURSE

**ORANGEBURG, SC (Exit 145 off I-26 to Hwy. 601 S.)**
**Telephone: (803)533-6030 Fax: (803)533-6032**

Head Pro: Tom Vargo - PGA
Course Supt.: Tom Vargo
Architect: Russell Breeden

18 - R - 6722 - 72

This course is noted for it's beautiful greens.
See pages 159-161 for "Tee-rific" Golf Package reservation details.

| | |
|---|---|
| $ | |
| Golf Pkgs. | Public |
| Power Carts | Lessons |
| Lounge | Snack Bar |
| | Open All Year |

Lakewood LINKS

## LINKS AT LAKEWOOD, THE

**SUMTER, SC. (Exit 108 off I-95 to Summerton, follow Hwy. 15 N. 25 Mi.)**
**Telephone: (803)481-5700**

Manager: Don Burchette
Head Pro: Don Burchette
Architect: Porter Gibson

18 - R - 6525 - 72

| | |
|---|---|
| $$ | |
| Golf Pkgs. | Public |
| Power Carts | Lessons |
| Lounge | Snack Bar |
| | Open All Year |

Water comes into play on 10 holes.
See pages 159-161 for "Tee-rific" Golf Package reservation details.

## NORTHWOODS GOLF CLUB

**COLUMBIA, SC (Exit I-20 on Farrow Rd., turn R., 2 Mi. to Carolina Research Park)**
**Telephone: (803)786-9242 Fax: (803)786-5033**

Manager: Greg McBride
Head Pro: Greg McBride - PGA
Course Supt.: Billy Ford
Architect: P.B. Dye

18 - R - 6550 - 72

| | |
|---|---|
| $$ | |
| Golf Pkgs. | Public |
| Power Carts | Lessons |
| Lounge | Snack Bar |
| Meals | Open All Year |

This course is a typical Dye course with many variations on types of holes.
See pages 159-161 for "Tee-rific" Golf Package reservation details.

# POCALLA SPRINGS COUNTRY CLUB

**SUMTER, SC (On Hwy. 15 South)**
**Telephone: (803)481-8322**

Head Pro: John Cain - PGA

18 - R - 5442 - 72

| | |
|---|---|
| $$ | |
| Golf Pkgs. | Public |
| Power Carts | Lessons |
| Lounge | Snack Bar |
| | Open All Year |

See pages 159-161 for "Tee-rific" Golf Package reservation details.

## PINELAND PLANTATION GOLF CLUB

**MAYESVILLE, SC (Exit #135, at I-95 & US 378)**
**Telephone: (803)495-3550 Or: (803)659-4359**

Owner: Guy M. Dabbs, Jr.
Head Pro: Jeff Schaffer
Course Supt.: Guy M. Dabbs, Jr.
Architect: Russell Breeden

18 - R - 6289 - 72

Set amidst a pine forest this course has 12 lakes on its property. Lots of Southern Hospitality is offered to all it's guests.

| | |
|---|---|
| $ | Resort |
| Golf Pkgs. | Public |
| Power Carts | Lessons |
| Lounge | Snack Bar |
| | Open All Year |

DRIVE CAREFULLY
Thank you for visiting ...
SOUTH CAROLINA
... Come again soon

# GOLF CONNECTIONS

# TENNESSEE

Pages 169-176

Springhouse G.C., Opryland Hotel

1992/93 DIRECTORY

# *Golf Vacations*

## TENNESSEE

Pages 169-176

GOLF CONNECTIONS

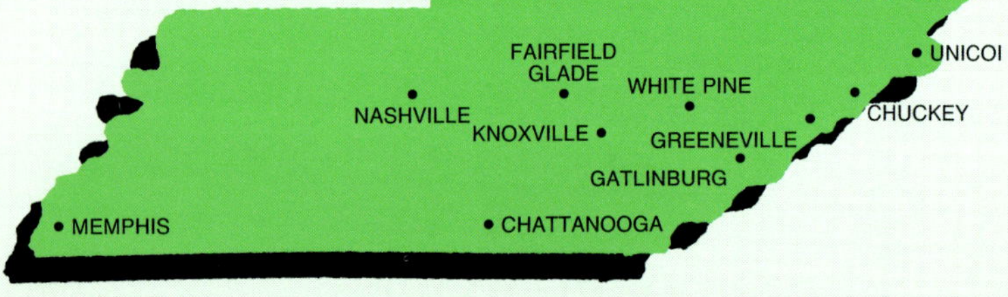


TENNESSEE

ANDREW JOHNSON GOLF CLUB

## ANDREW JOHNSON GOLF CLUB

**GREENEVILLE, TN. (On Lick Hollow Rd., off Hwy. 321)**
**Telephone: (615)636-1476 Toll Free: 1-800-421-2149**

Manager: Wilson Terry

18 Holes

The course offers Bermuda fairways and Bent grass greens.

| | |
|---|---|
| $ | |
| | Public |
| Power Carts | |
| | Snack Bar |
| | Open All Year |

Baneberry
Golf & Resort

## BANEBERRY GOLF & RESORT

**WHITE PINE, TN. (At the junction of I-81 and I-40)**
**Telephone: (615)674-2500**

Manager: Richard Kammann
Head Pro: Mitch Harmon

18 - R - 6707 - 71

A challenging course surrounded by Douglas Lake with a commanding view of the Great Smokies. A Baneberry golf vacation gives you the best of two worlds. A quiet mountain setting on a peaceful lake with many attractions nearby.Host of the $75,000 T.C. Jordan Golf Tour.

| | |
|---|---|
| $$ | Resort |
| Golf Pkgs. | Public |
| Power Carts | Lessons |
| Lounge | Snack Bar |
| Meals | Open All Year |

Bent Creek
GOLF RESORT

## BENT CREEK GOLF RESORT

**GATLINBURG, TN. (On Hwy. 321, 11 Mi. N. of Gatlinburg)**
**Telephone: (615)436-2875 US Toll Free: 1-800-251-9336**

Owner/Mgr.: James A. Calkin Jr.
Head Pro: Mark Wallace
Course Supt.: Don Clabo
Architect: Gary Player

18 - R - 6084 - 72

Golf course is set in the picturesque Greenbriar Valley 15 minutes away from Gatlinburg.

| | |
|---|---|
| $$ | Resort |
| Golf Pkgs. | Public |
| Power Carts | Lessons |
| Lounge | Snack Bar |
| Meals | Open All Year |

Buffalo Valley
Resort & C.C.

## BUFFALO VALLEY RESORT & COUNTRY CLUB

**UNICOI, TN. (N. of Unicoi on Hwy. 23)**
**Telephone: (615)743-5021 Toll Free: 1-800-882-0096**

Manager: Bob Wolfe

18 - R - 7000 - 72

Home course of the East Tennessee State University.
Course set in the scenic beauty of mountains, lakes and rivers.

| | |
|---|---|
| $$ | Resort |
| Golf Pkgs. | Public |
| Power Carts | Lessons |
| Lounge | Snack Bar |
| Meals | Open All Year |

## FALL CREEK FALLS STATE PARK GOLF COURSE

**PIKEVILLE, TN (State Hwy. #30)**
**Telephone: (615)881-5706**

Owner: State of Tennessee
Head Pro: Billy Maxwell
Architect: Joe Lee

18 - R - 6378 - 72

This course has northern bluegrass fairways and bent grass greens and features many dogleg holes synonymous with a Joe Lee design.

| | |
|---|---|
| $ | |
| Golf Pkgs. | Public |
| Power Carts | Lessons |
| | Snack Bar |
| Meals | Open All Year |



## GRAYSBURG HILLS GOLF COURSE

**CHUKEY, TN. (12 Mi. N/E of Greeneville, on State Rte. 93)**
**Telephone: (615)234-8061**

Owner/Mgr.: Fred Stewart
Architect: Rees Jones

18 - R - 6804 - 72

One of the top public golf facilities in Tennessee. A quiet setting surrounds this challenging yet enjoyable course with its 60 sand bunkers and strategically located water hazards. Golf packages available with Days Inn.
SEE OUR FULL PAGE AD ON NEXT PAGE.

| | |
|---|---|
| $$ | |
| Golf Pkgs. | Public |
| Power Carts | Lessons |
| Lounge | Snack Bar |
| | Open All Year |

## GATLINBURG COUNTRY CLUB

**PIGEON FORGE, TN (On Dollywood Lane)**
**Telephone: (615)453-3912 Fax: (615)453-8099**

Owner: City of Gatlinburg
Head Pro: Harry A. (Cotton) Berrier
Course Supt.: Jeff Rumph
Architect: William B. Langford

18 - R - 6281 - 72

Located in the foothills of the Great Smoky Mountains this course offers breathtaking views as well as challenging golf. Hole #12 is one of the most picturesque holes in the country. It is 194 yds. in length and drops 200 ft. straight down.

| | |
|---|---|
| $$ | |
| | Public |
| Power Carts | Lessons |
| Lounge | Snack Bar |
| | Open All Year |

## HENRY HORTON STATE PARK GOLF COURSE

**CHAPEL HILL, TN (Exit #46 from I-65 S. and follow the signs)**
**Telephone: (615)364-2319**

Owner: State of Tennessee
Head Pro: Kerry Blanton

18 - R - 6580 - 72

This course features large bent grass greens and hybrid bermuda fairways gently contoured and cut through hardwood forests.Hole #18 is one of the longest in Tennessee - a full 615 yards from the championship tees.

| | |
|---|---|
| $ | |
| Golf Pkgs. | Public |
| Power Carts | Lessons |
| | Snack Bar |
| Meals | Open All Year |

## MONTGOMERY BELL STATE PARK GOLF COURSE

**BURNS, TN (On Hwy. 47, take I-40 W. from Nashville, 40 Miles, follow the signs)**
**Telephone: (615)797-2578**

Owner: State of Tennessee
Head Pro: Darryl Hartsfield
Architect: Gary Rodger Baird

18 - R - 6065 - 72

Be sure to play this course in the spring for the best view of the myriads of dogwood trees all over the course. Large, contured bent grass greens are surrounded by mounds. Hybrid Bermuda fairways.

| | |
|---|---|
| $ | |
| Golf Pkgs. | Public |
| Power Carts | Lessons |
| | Snack Bar |
| Meals | Open All Year |

## SPRINGHOUSE GOLF CLUB

**NASHVILLE, TN. (1-1/2 Mi. from Opryland Hotel with shuttle service every 1/2 hr.)**
**Telephone: (615)871-7759 Fax: (615)871-5906**

Director of Golf: Chuck Eade
Head Pro: Neil Collins
Course Supt.: Andrew Brennan
Architect: Larry Nelson

18 - R - 5788 - 72
Scottish Links layout bordered by the Cumberland River and a 100 foot limestone bluff. The course plays from 5000 yards to over 7000 yards from five different sets of tees.

| | |
|---|---|
| $$$ | Resort |
| Golf Pkgs. | Public |
| Power Carts | Lessons |
| Lounge | Snack Bar |
| Meals | Open All Year |

## PARIS LANDING STATE PARK GOLF COURSE

**BUCHANAN, TN (On US 79)**
**Telephone: (901)644-1332**

Owner: State of Tennessee
Head Pro: Keith Hickman

18 - R - 6479 - 72

This very contoured course is cut out of a hardwood forest with several holes bordering on Kentucky Lake. The signature hole is number 4, a 182-yd. par 3, with a beautiful vista overlooking the lake. Bent grass greens.

| | |
|---|---|
| $ | |
| Golf Pkgs. | Public |
| Power Carts | Lessons |
| | Snack Bar |
| Meals | Open All Year |

## PICKWICK LANDING STATE PARK GOLF COURSE

**PICKWICK DAM, TN (On State Hwy. 57)**
**Telephone: (901)689-3149**

Owner: State of Tennessee
Head Pro: Reg Scott

18 - R - 6401 - 72

This course features hybrid bermuda greens and fairways. There are several challenging dogleg holes, the No. 1 handicap hole being number 2, a 371-yd. par 4, with a difficult second shot to the green.

| | |
|---|---|
| $ | |
| Golf Pkgs. | Public |
| Power Carts | Lessons |
| | Snack Bar |
| Meals | Open All Year |

Stonehenge
GOLF • CLUB

## STONEHENGE GOLF CLUB

**FAIRFIELD GLADE, TN (Just off I-40, between Nashville and Knoxville.)**
**Telephone: (615)484-7521 Fax: (615)484-3788**

Owner: Fairfield Communities, Inc.
Head Pro: Tom Waltz
Course Supt.: Brian Holland
Architect: Joe Lee

18 - R - 6549 - 72

Stonehenge features bent gress tees, greens and fairways. It was *Golf Digest's* "Best New Course" in 1985, and is listed in the top 75 courses in the counrty. See page 171 for "Fairway Packages".

| | |
|---|---|
| $$$ | Resort |
| Golf Pkgs. | Public |
| Power Carts | Lessons |
| Lounge | Snack Bar |
| Meals | Open All Year |

GOLF

GOLF CONNECTIONS

# VIRGINIA

Pages 177-184

Winter Green G.C.

1992/93 DIRECTORY

# *Golf Vacations*

## VIRGINIA

Pages 177-184

GOLF CONNECTIONS

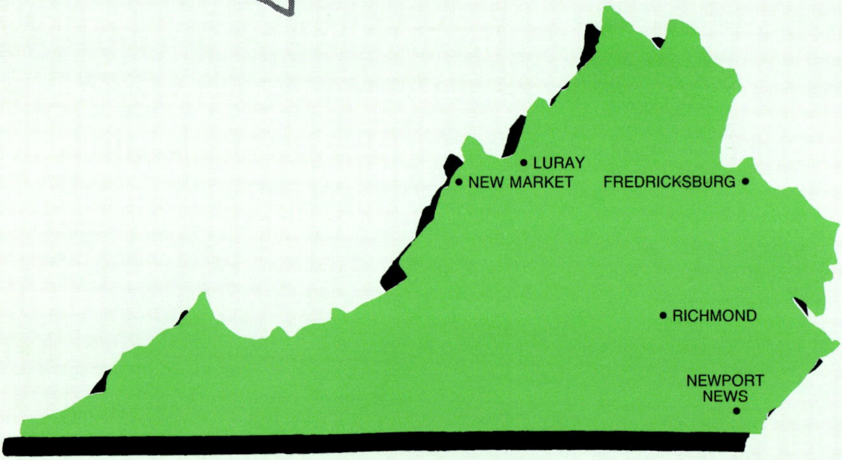


VIRGINIA

# Virginia is for Lovers Golf Lovers that is !!!

Site of some of the nation's premier Revolutionary and Civil Wars, Virginia is a microcosm of America in terms of its four centuries of history and its widely varying geography.

But Virginia is also a lush green haven for golf and the quality of golf in Virginia has always been nothing short of outstanding.

Its extraordinary natural beauty encompasses the Atlantic Ocean, Chesapeake Bay, numerous rivers and lakes and mountains with spectacular views.

Steeped in history, Virginia offers some of the best of the old and new in golf. Here golfers can find the nation's oldest first tee still in use at the Homestead course in Hot Springs. They can also experience some of the most exciting new courses that have gained national and international recognition for design.

Golfers with varied sporting interests can even golf and ski on the same day at Wintergreen Resort in the Blue Ridge Mountains.

With more than135 public, semi-private and resort courses available from one end of the state to the other you will find Virginia golf to be simply an outstanding golf value.

Virginia is home to golf legend Sam Snead and two-time U.S. Open winner Curtis Strange, (among a host of other on the P.G.A. Tour) and you are invited to make it your vacation home away from home.

But be careful. As a golfer you might just fall in love . . . with Virginia.

FOR MORE INFORMATION CONTACT:

Virginia Division of Tourism

1021 East Cary St. Richmond, VA 23219

**1-800-93BACK9**

## BRYCE RESORT

**BASYE, VA (On Hwy. 263 W., from exit 273 off I-81)**
**Telephone: (703)856-2121**

Head Pro: Gregg Bowman
Course Supt.: Roger Schmitt
Architect: Ed Ault

18 - R - 6024 - 71

Built along the beautiful mountains in the Shenandoah Valley. Tight fairways cross water on 10 holes. Power carts are mandatory.

| | |
|---|---|
| $$ | Resort |
| Golf Pkgs. | |
| Power Carts | Lessons |
| Lounge | Snack Bar |
| Meals | Open All Year |

## CAVERNS COUNTRY CLUB RESORT

**LURAY, VA (Airport exit from US 211, 1 Mi. W. of Luray)**
**Telephone: (703)743-7111**

Owner: Luray Caverns
Head Pro: Breck Johnson
Course Supt.: Michael Ketchum
Architect: Mal Purdy

18 - R - 6452 - 72

Gently rolling fairways with large trees and bent grass greens. Magnificent setting. World famous Luray Caverns are nearby.

| | |
|---|---|
| $$ | Resort |
| Golf Pkgs. | Public |
| Power Carts | |
| | Snack Bar |
| | Open All Year |

## KILN CREEK GOLF & COUNTRY CLUB

**NEWPORT NEWS, VA (On Brick Kiln Rd., E. off I-64 at exit 255B, Jefferson Ave.)**
**Telephone: (804)874-2600**

Course Supt.: Dave Harmon
Architect: Tom Clark

18 - R - 6357 - 72
Rating: Men's - 70.1 / Slope 125

This course has been rated as one of the top 100 new courses in America by GOLF DIGEST. It is modeled in keeping with the great links of Scotland.

| | |
|---|---|
| $$ | Resort |
| Golf Pkgs. | Public |
| Power Carts | Lessons |
| Lounge | Snack Bar |
| Meals | Open All Year |

*In the Heart of the Shenandoah Valley*
*in the Midst of the Blue Ridge Mountains*

# The SHENVALEE

Visit SHENVALEE and discover enjoyable, relaxing golf in the beautiful and historical Shenandoah Valley. Set in the midst of the picturesque Blue Ridge Mountains of Virginia, it offers all you need for a memorable golf vacation.

True to its history, SHENVALEE's beautifully maintained and uniquely designed 18 hole PGA course first opened to the public in 1927. Its front nine was built by a large force of men wielding picks and shovels and using horse-drawn wagons to transport dirt. The back nine holes were added in 1963.

Here hospitality is a way of life. Fine dining in an elegant restaurant with delicious food and warm ambiance, a quiet drink in the "Sand Trap Tavern" and graciously appointed rooms - poolside or overlooking the golf course.

- EXCELLENT GOLF PACKAGES -

Two day to seven day packages are very reasonable and special mid-week packages are even less.

FOR MORE INFORMATION CONTACT:

## THE SHENVALEE GOLF RESORT

P.O. Box 430, New Market, Virginia 22844
Tel: (703) 740-3181 • Fax: (703) 740-8931

## THE SHENVALEE GOLF RESORT

**NEW MARKET, VA (Follow signs from exit 264 at I-81)**
**Telephone: (703)740-3181 Fax: (703)740-8931**

General Manager: Edy Orebaugh

18 - R - 5657 - 70

In the Heart of the Shenandoah Valley in the midst of the Blue Ridge Mountains. Unique in design and beautifully maintained.

| | |
|---|---|
| $$ | Resort |
| Golf Pkgs. | Public |
| Power Carts | Lessons |
| Lounge | Snack Bar |
| Meals | Open All Year |

# Shannon Green Golf Club

## Four Leaf Clover Golf Package

**$264** per person / double occupancy

Includes:

• Two nights hotel accommodations • Welcome cocktail in Shannons Lounge • Two full breakfasts • Two dinners • Three days unlimited golf green fees • Three days cart rental - 18 holes per day • Souvenir bag tag • Two buckets of range balls • Sleeve of Shannon Green golf balls • All taxes and gratuities

Centrally located on Interstate 95 less than one hour south of Washington D.C. and 50 minutes north of Richmond, Virginia at exit 130B. This 18 hole par 72 championship test is set amid Virginia farmland with rolling terrain and a combination of water and trees. The course measures 5751 from the forward tees to 7155 from the championship tees.

The Sheraton is a full service conference facility with 11500 square feet of meeting space. Casual dining in the Meadows Restaurant or the Greens Tavern and live entertainment in Shannons Lounge. On over 300 acres you will find three outdoor tennis courts, junior-Olympic size swimming pool, basketball, volleyball, horseshoes, shuffleboard, driving range and practice putting green. Only three miles from Fredericksburgh's 40-block National Historic District and Civil War Battlefields.

To receive more information or make reservations call:

**1-800-682-1049**

**Sheraton Inn Fredericksburg**

**CONFERENCE CENTER**

2801 PLANK ROAD, P.O. BOX 618, FREDERICKSBURG, VA 22404
PHONE: (703) 786-8321 FAX: (703) 786-3957

ITT Sheraton. The Natural Choice

# Sheraton Inn Harrisonburg

The hospitality people of ITT

OFFERS

## UNLIMITED 3 DAY GOLF PACKAGE

**Including:**

- **Two Nights Lodging**
- **Two Dinners**
- **Two Breakfasts**
- **Hors d'Oeuvres**
- **Three Days Unlimited Golf**
- **Golf Cart (for 1st. eighteen holes each day)**

---

LAKEVIEW GOLF COURSE

Located only minutes away, nestled in the Shenandoah Valley in the shadows of the Blue Ridge & Massanutten Mountains are 6500 yards of gently rolling fairways that present a challenge to the seasoned golfer and offer an enjoyable experience to the weekend player.

Large tees and greens compliment this 18 hole par 72 championship course. An additional nine holes are available for your enjoyment.

---

Following golf ....

- Indoor/Outdoor Heated Swimming Pools • Jacuzzi
- Sauna • Hiking • Caverns • Fishing • Horseback Riding
- Antique Malls & Outlet Shopping (only minutes away)

---

*- ADVANCE RESERVATIONS ARE RECOMMENDED -*

For more information contact:

**Alice L. Reichard** - Asst. Gen. Mgr.

**Tel: (703) 433-2521 Fax: (703) 434-0253**

1400 East Market St. Harrisonburg, Virginia 22801

## WINTERGREEN RESORT

**WINTERGREEN, VA (Exit off I-81)**

**Telephone: (804)325-2200 Toll Free: 1-800-325-2200**

Owner/Mgr.: Gunter Muller
Head Pro: David Jimenez
Course Supt.: Robert Ruff
Architects: Ellis Maples/Rees Jones

36 Holes: Devil's Knob: 18 - R - 6576 - 70
Stoney Creek: 18 - R - 7005 - 72

Stoney Creek is rated #2 in Virginia by *Golf Digest*. Devil's Knob is rated in Virginia's top ten. Wintergreen is home to the Highlander Golf Academy.

| | |
|---|---|
| $$$ | Resort |
| Golf Pkgs. | Public |
| Power Carts | Lessons |
| Lounge | Snack Bar |
| Meals | Open All Year |

# GOLF CONNECTIONS

# WEST VIRGINIA

Pages 185-192

Speidel Golf Course, Oglebay, Wheeling, West Virginia

1992/93 DIRECTORY

# Golf Vacations

## WEST VIRGINIA

Pages 185-192

GOLF CONNECTIONS

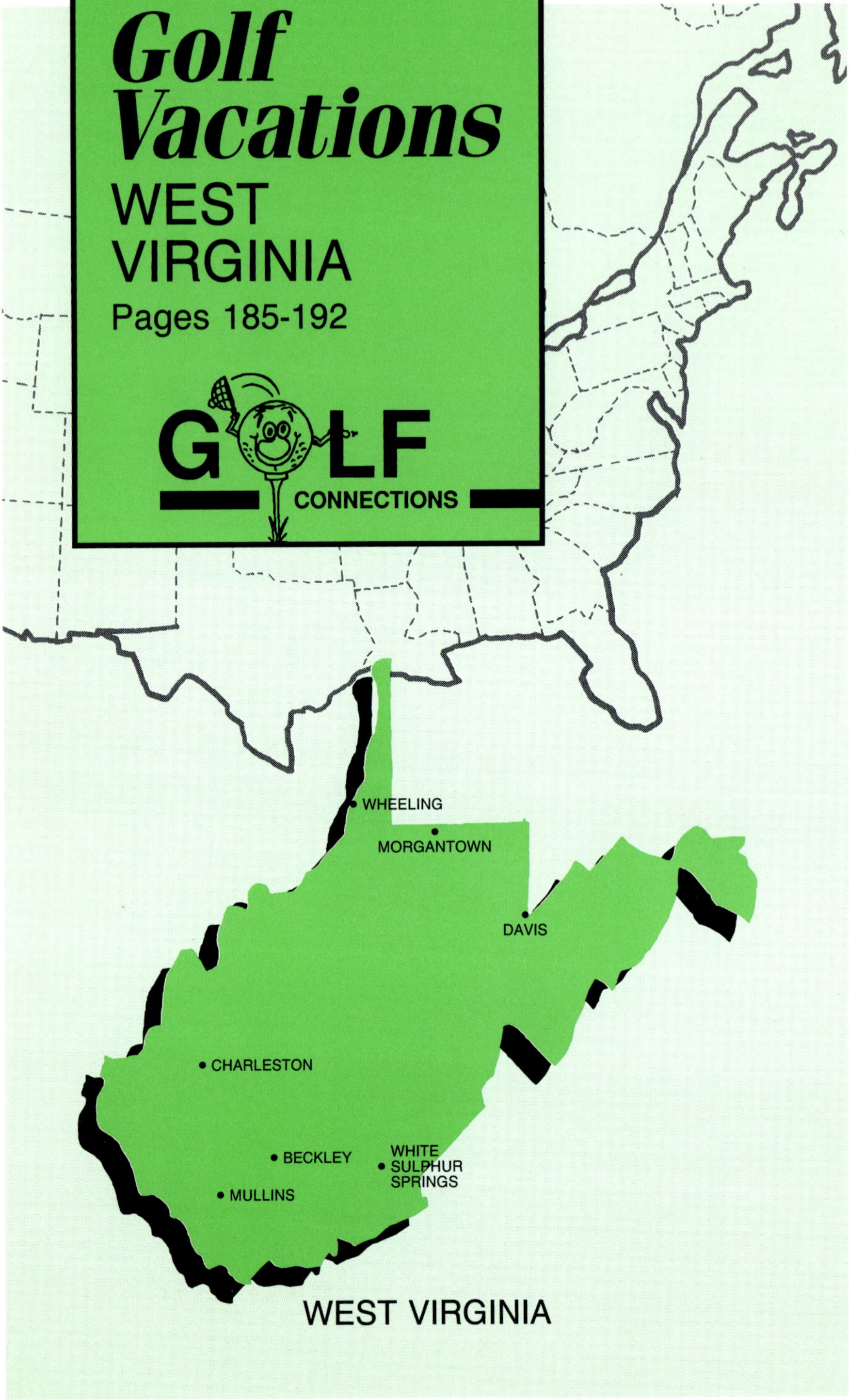

Southern
West Virginia
is 'FORE'...
GOLFERS

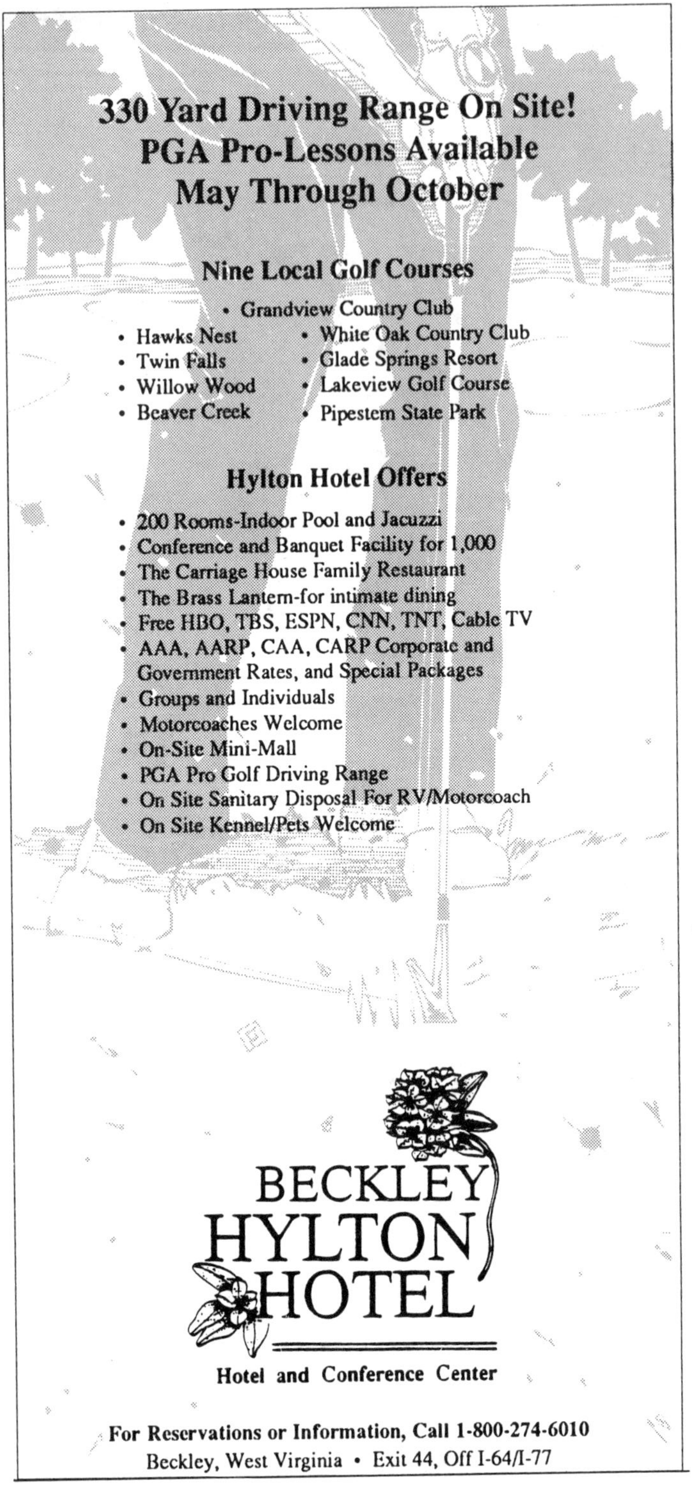
330 Yard Driving Range On Site!
PGA Pro-Lessons Available
May Through October
Nine Local Golf Courses
• Grandview Country Club
• Hawks Nest
• Twin Falls
• Willow Wood
• Beaver Creek
• White Oak Country Club
• Glade Springs Resort
• Lakeview Golf Course
• Pipestem State Park
Hylton Hotel Offers
• 200 Rooms-Indoor Pool and Jacuzzi
• Conference and Banquet Facility for 1,000
• The Carriage House Family Restaurant
• The Brass Lantern-for intimate dining
• Free HBO, TBS, ESPN, CNN, TNT, Cable TV
• AAA, AARP, CAA, CARP Corporate and Government Rates, and Special Packages
• Groups and Individuals
• Motorcoaches Welcome
• On-Site Mini-Mall
• PGA Pro Golf Driving Range
• On Site Sanitary Disposal For RV/Motorcoach
• On Site Kennel/Pets Welcome
BECKLEY
HYLTON
HOTEL
Hotel and Conference Center
For Reservations or Information, Call 1-800-274-6010
Beckley, West Virginia • Exit 44, Off I-64/I-77

CANAAN VALLEY
Resort & Conference Center
A WEST VIRGINIA STATE PARK

## CANAAN VALLEY RESORT

**DAVIS, WV (On Hwy. 32, south of Davis and north of Harman)**
**Telephone:(304)866-4121 or: 800-225-5982**

Owner: West Virginia State Parks
Head Pro: Bud Harold
Architect: Godfrey Cornish

18 - R - 6436 - 72

Breathtaking vistas and gentle rolling terrain. Cool summertime temperatures and low humidity, coupled with excellent playing conditions on this carefully manicured course makes for the ultimate golfing experience.

| | |
|---|---|
| $$ | Resort |
| Golf Pkgs. | Public |
| Power Carts | Lessons |
| Lounge | Snack Bar |
| Meals | Open All Year |

Glade Springs

## GLADE SPRINGS RESORT

**DANIELS, WV (At intersection of I-64 & I-77 near Beckley WV)**
**Telephone: (304)763-2000 Toll Free: 1-800-634-5233**

Manager: Jeff Halpin
Head Pro: Steve Hazelwood
Course Supt.: Rodney Noel
Architect: George Cobb

18 - R - 61176 - 72

Very large greens and eight lakes on the course. Full service clubhouse. Glade Springs is a 4000 acre estate, resort and conference center.

| | |
|---|---|
| $$$ | Resort |
| Golf Pkgs. | Public |
| Power Carts | Lessons |
| Lounge | Snack Bar |
| Meals | Open All Year |

## CRISPIN GOLF COURSE

**WHEELING, WV (At Oglebay, on Interstate 70, off I-79 south of Pittsburgh)**
**Tel: (304)243-4090** **Canada Toll Free: 1-800-633-9975**
**U.S.A. Toll Free: 1-800-624-6988**

| | |
|---|---|
| $$ | Resort |
| Golf Pkgs. | Public |
| Power Carts | Lessons |
| Lounge | Snack Bar |
| Meals | Open All Year |

Head Pro: Karen Waialae
Architect: Robert Biery

18 - R - 5670 - 71
Rating: Men's - 66.6

This natural course traverses the beautiful Wesy Virginia hills and offers the golfer ever-changing views of Oglebay.

## TWIN FALLS RESORT STATE PARK

**MULLENS, WV (5.5 mi. from Maben, off W.V. Rte 97, left at Bear Hole Rd. )**
**Telephone: (304)294-4000**

| | |
|---|---|
| $ | Resort |
| Golf Pkgs. | Public |
| Power Carts | Lessons |
| | Snack Bar |
| Meals | Open All Year |

Manager:A. Scott Durham, Supt.
Head Pro: Joe Comer
Course Architects: Geoffrey Cornish/George Cobb

18 - R - 5977 - 71 Rating: 70.1

Bent grass greens and bluegrass fairways set amidst a beautiful state park. Accomodations available at Twin Falls Lodge, Cottages, and Campground.

## SPEIDEL GOLF COURSE

**WHEELING, WV (At Oglebay, on Interstate 70 off I-79 south of Pittsburgh)**
**Canada: 800-633-9975 U.S.A.: 800-624-6988**

Head Pro: Karen Waialae
Course Supt.: Ed Murphy
Architect: Robert Trent Jones

18 - R - 7000 - 71

| | |
|---|---|
| $$ | Resort |
| Golf Pkgs. | Public |
| Power Carts | Lessons |
| Lounge | Snack Bar |
| Meals | |

Ranked by *Golf Digest* as one of America's best public golf courses. Multiple tee placements for all levels of play. Beautiful course.

DRIVE CAREFULLY
Thank you for visiting ...
WEST VIRGINIA
... Come again soon

GOLF CONNECTIONS

# ISLAND GOLF

Pages 193-203

Atlantik Beach Resort, Lucaya, Grand Bahamas

1992/93 DIRECTORY

# Golf Vacations

## ISLAND GOLF

Pages 193-203

GOLF CONNECTIONS

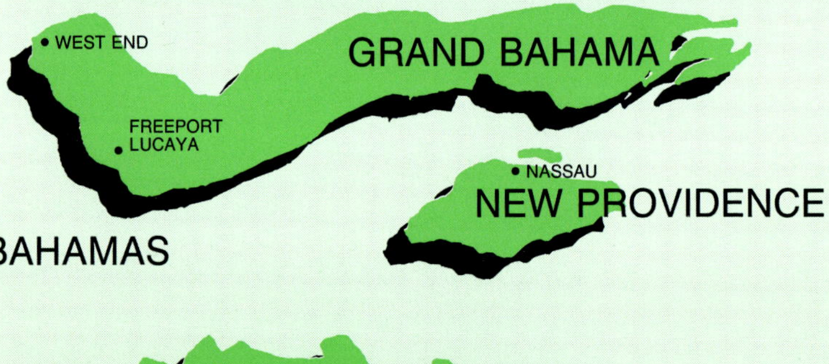


BAHAMAS

U.S. VIRGIN ISLANDS

***The Bahamas boasts*** some of the best professionally designed golf courses in the world. These include PGA championship courses designed by the likes of Dick Wilson, Joe Lee, Mark Mahannah and Robert Trent Jones. When you play our courses, you join the list of some of the best pros in the game.

You can have the quiet of our Family Islands such as Abaco and Eleuthera. Or choose the excitement and nightlife of Freeport or Nassau. Experience it all in the Bahamas.

## *It's Better in The Bahamas*

### *Even the Color is Better in the Bahamas*

*When the jet decends from the boundless blue sky and allows you a first glimpse of Nassau, Freeport or The Family Islands, you'll think that, until now, you've been watching everthing in black and white, that your life has been in monochrome and now, suddenly, a giant box of crayons has exploded right in your face.*

*There are a hundred vibrant blues, maybe more, in the ocean's reflection. Another hundred hues of green are in the trees and other flora. The vivid colors of the taxicabs and hotels and cruise ships . . . powerful reds and blues, dynamic pinks and fluorescent purples . . . paint an image so strong that it seems almost shocking. The pastels that color the other buildings, even the humblest residence, fill your senses with more calming, but no less moving stimulation.*

*You needn't be a pro to play on our GREENS, but if you are, you'll feel right at home. The climate, the ambiance and the challenge will be available to you all year round. Welcome to the Bahamas !!!*

## LUCAYA GOLF & COUNTRY CLUB

**FREEPORT, LUCAYA, GRAND BAHAMA**
**Telephone: (809)373-1066**

Owners: Atlantik Beach Resort
Golf Co-Ordinator/Course Supt.: Robert Paisley
Head Pro: Max Russell
Architect: Dick Wilson

18 - CH - 6824 - 72

Fairways are lined with pine trees and dense underbrush. Elevated and well bunkered greens. One of the best manicured courses on Grand Bahama Island.

| | |
|---|---|
| $$$ | Resort |
| Golf Pkgs. | Public |
| Power Carts | Lessons |
| Lounge | Snack Bar |
| Meals | Open All Year |

## BAHAMAS PRINCESS RESORT & CASINO

### FREEPORT, GRAND BAHAMAS — EMERALD COURSE

**Telephone: (809)352-9661 US Toll FRee: 1-800-223-1834**

Owners: Princess Hotels International Inc.
Golf Manager: Laura Godet
Head Pros: Ben Stuart/Hartley Pinder
Architect: Dick Wilson

18 - R - 6420 - 72

The 9th hole, a 545 yard per 5 is considered one of the best in the Bahamas. Site of the PGA Bahamas National Open in 1970

| | |
|---|---|
| $$$ | Resort |
| Golf Pkgs. | Public |
| Power Carts | Lessons |
| Lounge | Snack Bar |
| Meals | Open All Year |

## BAHAMAS PRINCESS RESORT & CASINO

### FREEPORT, GRAND BAHAMAS — RUBY COURSE

**Telephone: (809)352-9661 US Toll FRee: 1-800-223-1834**

Owners: Princess Hotels International Inc.
Golf Manager: Laura Godet
Head Pros: Ben Stuart/Hartley Pinder
Architect: Joe Lee

18 - R - 6515 - 72

Lush Bermuda fairways lined by tall arawak pines, along with over 200 other species of fauna, many of them flowering, to hide errant tee shots or to provide some beautiful views. The par 3 holes are considered a stern test of golf skill.

| | |
|---|---|
| $$$ | Resort |
| Golf Pkgs. | Public |
| Power Carts | Lessons |
| Lounge | Snack Bar |
| Meals | Open All Year |

## COTTON BAY CLUB

**ROCK SOUND, ELEUTHERA, BAHAMAS**
**Telephone: (809)334-6156**

Manager: Ron Lindemann
Architect: Robert Trent Jones, Sr.

18 - R - 7068 - 72

| | |
|---|---|
| $$$ | Resort |
| Golf Pkgs. | Public |
| Power Carts | Lessons |
| Lounge | Snack Bar |
| Meals | |

If there is a golf shrine in the Bahamas, this is it.

Paradise Island Golf Club
PARADISE ISLAND, BAHAMAS

## PARADISE ISLAND GOLF COURSE

**NASSAU, BAHAMAS**
**Telephone: (809)363-3925** **US Toll Free: 1-800-722-7466**

Owner: Resorts International
Director of Golf: Fred Higgs
Architect: Dick Wilson

18 - R - 6700 - 72

| | |
|---|---|
| $$$ | Resort |
| Golf Pkgs. | Public |
| Power Carts | Lessons |
| Lounge | Snack Bar |
| Meals | Open All Year |

Specially constructed to compliment its tropical setting, this course is bordered on three sides by the Atlantic Ocean. Holes number 6 and 7 are of particular beauty and challenge.

## RAMADA SOUTH OCEAN GOLF & BEACH RESORT

**SOUTH OCEAN, NASSAU, BAHAMAS**
**Telephone: (809)362-4391**

Director of Golf: Carl Marinello
Course Supt.: Alonzo Hamilton
Architect: Joe Lee

18 - R - 6707 - 72

A picturesque course with undulating greens, and the toughest back nine on the island. FORMERLY THE DIVI BAHAMAS.

| | |
|---|---|
| $$$ | Resort |
| Golf Pkgs. | Public |
| Power Carts | Lessons |
| Lounge | Snack Bar |
| Meals | Open All Year |

## RIVIERA RESORT & COUNTRY CLUB

**CABLE BEACH, NASSAU, BAHAMAS**
**Telephone: (809)327-6200** **US Toll Free: 1-800-222-7466**

Owner: Riviera Resorts
Director of Golf: Vernon Lockhart
Head Pro: Richard Gibson
Architect: James McCormick
18 - R - 6534 - 72

The oldest course in the Bahamas. Rolling fairways lined with coconut palms, and casuarina pines. Fairways, traps and water hazards srategically placed. FORMERLY CARNIVAL'S CRYSTAL PALACE GOLF CLUB

| | |
|---|---|
| $$$ | Resort |
| Golf Pkgs. | Public |
| Power Carts | Lessons |
| Lounge | Snack Bar |
| Meals | Open All Year |

**MAHOGANY RUN** *is one of the lovliest and most naturally beautiful golf resorts anywhere in the world.*

*This storied course rises and drops like a roller coaster on its journey to the sea where spectacular cliffs and crashing seas are the ultimate hazards at the* ***13th*** *and* ***14th*** *holes. As a matter of fact* ***#14*** *is too breathtaking to warrant scoring, between the tee and green there is nothing but the surf of the turquoise sea.*

*Small greens, tight fairways and tradewinds are the challenge, and accuracy, not distance is called for. GOLF MAGAZINE said "There are 18 excellent reasons for golfers to visit St. Thomas, all at Mahogany Run."*

***MAHOGANY RUN's 18 holes*** *were designed by George and Tom Fazio in one of the most beautiful spots in the Carribean for a golf course. The hills and valleys of St. Thomas, along with its beautiful coastline and colourful flora, make this golf course one of the most memorable you'll play.*

*See photo on the inside back cover of this directory.*

## MAHOGANY RUN GOLF & TENNIS RESORT

**ST. THOMAS, US VIRGIN ISLANDS**
**Telephone: (809)775-5000 Fax: (809)775-1556**

Manager: John Russo
Head Pro: Nevin Phillips
Course Supt.:Herbert Lewis
Architect: George & Tom Fazio

18 - R - 6022 - 70

Home of the famous "Devil's Triangle". If the toughness of holes #13, #14 and #15 doesn't thrill you, their beauty will.

| | |
|---|---|
| $$$ | Resort |
| Golf Pkgs. | Public |
| Power Carts | Lessons |
| Lounge | Snack Bar |
| Meals | Open All Year |

# Bermuda
## Department of Tourism

1200 Bay Street, Suite 1004, Toronto, Ontario M5R 2A5
Phone (416) 923-9600 • Fax (416) 923-4840

**BERMUDA . . .**
A short trip to the perfect golf holiday !!

Bermuda has more golf courses per square mile than any other country in the world which means you will never have to travel too far to tee off.

With a great variety of properties to choose from Bermuda is not only affordable but accessible

Only 2-1/2 hours from Toronto you can be on the fairways of some of the worlds most challenging golf courses

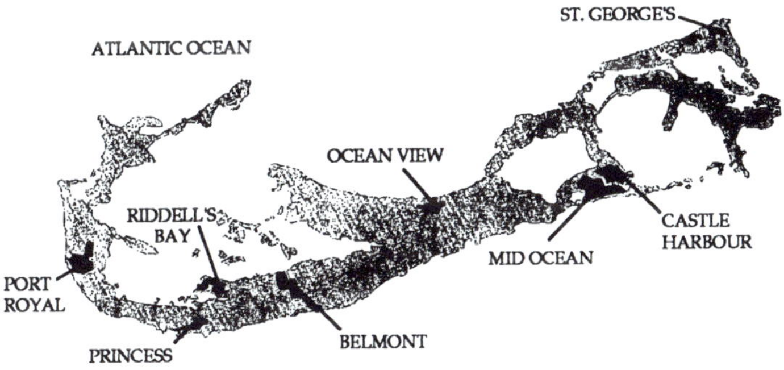


**No matter where you stay,
a chip and a putt puts you on any one
of our 8 championship courses.**

## BELMONT GOLF & COUNTRY CLUB

**WARWICK PARISH, BERMUDA**

**Telephone: (809)236-1301 Toll Free: 1-800-225-5843**

Owner: Trusthouse Forte International Hotels
Dir. of Golf: Ian Crowe
Head Pro: Cornell Bean

18 - R - 5745 - 70

| | |
|---|---|
| $$ | Resort |
| Golf Pkgs. | Public |
| Power Carts | Lessons |
| Lounge | Snack Bar |
| Meals | Open All Year |

Elevated and double tiered greens, tight fairways and small, narrow putting surfaces make Belmont one of the most challenging on the Island.

## CASTLE HARBOUR GOLF CLUB

**HAMILTON PARISH, BERMUDA**

**Telephone: (809)293-2040 ext.:6670**

Dir. of Golf: Bruce Fraser
Head Pro: Kevin Benevides
Architects: Charles Banks/Robert Trent Jones

18 - R - 6640 - 71

| | |
|---|---|
| $$$ | Resort |
| Golf Pkgs. | Public |
| Power Carts | Lessons |
| Lounge | Snack Bar |
| Meals | Open All Year |

The view from the first tee is magnificent. This course demands precise tee shots and accurate irons into heavily trapped greens.

## MID OCEAN GOLF CLUB

**TUCKER'S TOWN, BERMUDA**

**Telephone: (809)293-0330**

Head Pro: Keith Pearman

18 - R - 6547 - 72

Introduction by members required at this private course.
Ranked by experts as one of the top links style courses in the world.

## OCEAN VIEW GOLF & COUNTRY CLUB

**DEVONSHIRE PARISH, BERMUDA**

**Telephone: (809)292-6758**

Owner: Bermuda Government
Manager: Wendell Tucker
Head Pro: Roger Outerbridge

9 - R - 2956 - 35

| | |
|---|---|
| $$ | Resort |
| Golf Pkgs. | Public |
| Power Carts | Lessons |
| Lounge | Snack Bar |
| Meals | Open All Year |

Unpredictable terrain and rambling hills make this course doggedly resistant to low scoring.

## PORT ROYAL GOLF COURSE

**SOUTHAMPTON PARISH, BERMUDA**

**Start Times: (809)234-0974 Pro Shop: (809)234-0972**

Owner: Bermuda Government
Manager: Max Atherden
Head Pro: Francis Rabain
Architect: Robert Trent Jones

18 - R - 6425 - 71

Well trapped greens and bunkered fairways will demand your full attention.

| | |
|---|---|
| $$ | |
| Golf Pkgs. | Public |
| Power Carts | Lessons |
| Lounge | Snack Bar |
| Meals | Open All Year |

## PRINCESS GOLF CLUB

**SOUTHAMPTON PARISH, BERMUDA**

**Telephone: (809)238-0446**

Dir. of Golf: Bruce Sims
Head Pro: Ron Wallace

18 - R - 5439 - 68

A deceptive 18 hole par 3 course. It demands accuracy and skill for the irons. Lots of water and elevated tees.

| | |
|---|---|
| $$ | Resort |
| Golf Pkgs. | Public |
| Power Carts | Lessons |
| Lounge | Snack Bar |
| Meals | Open All Year |

## RIDDELL'S BAY GOLF & COUNTRY CLUB

**WARWICK PARISH, BERMUDA**

**Telephone: (809)238-1060**

Head Pro: Darron Swan

18 - R - 5439 - 68

The "senior" of Bermuda country clubs this course has been in operation since 1922. Tight fairways and small narrow greens.

## ST. GEORGE'S GOLF CLUB

**ST. GEORGE'S PARISH, BERMUDA**

**Telephone: (809)297-8067**

Owner: Bermuda Government
Mgr./Head Pro: Kim Swan
Architect: Robert Trent Jones

18 - Ex. - 4502 - 64

On this new course, opened in 1985, the major factor is wind. 9 iron to a driver required on par 3's depending on the weather.

| | |
|---|---|
| $ | |
| Golf Pkgs. | Public |
| Power Carts | Lessons |
| Lounge | Snack Bar |
| Meals | Open All Year |

. . "TWO SEATS TOGETHER, ONE FOR MY CLUBS, NEAR THE DOOR!"

Bayme adows GOLF CLUB

***JACKSONVILLE, FL***

(See page 33 for details on facility)

**1 COMPLIMENTARY BUCKET OF RANGE BALLS**
FOR EVERY ROUND OF 18 HOLES OF GOLF

ONE VOUCHER PER PERSON

. . . . . . . . . . . . . . . .
Validation

**DO NOT DETACH VOUCHERS FROM THE BOOK**

***BOBBY JONES GOLF COMPLEX***
***AMERICAN COURSE***

***SARASOTA, FL***

(See page 34 for details on facility)

**1 COMPLIMENTARY LARGE BUCKET OF RANGE BALLS**
FOR EVERY ROUND OF 18 HOLES OF GOLF WITH POWER CART

ONE VOUCHER PER PERSON

. . . . . . . . . . . . . . . .
Validation

**DO NOT DETACH VOUCHERS FROM THE BOOK**

***BOBBY JONES GOLF COMPLEX***
***BRITISH COURSE***

***SARASOTA, FL***

(See page 34 for details on facility)

**1 COMPLIMENTARY LARGE BUCKET OF RANGE BALLS**
FOR EVERY ROUND OF 18 HOLES OF GOLF WITH POWER CART

ONE VOUCHER PER PERSON

. . . . . . . . . . . . . . . .
Validation

**DO NOT DETACH VOUCHERS FROM THE BOOK**

**Grenelefe**
**Resort & Conference Center**

***HAINES CITY, FL***

(See page 38 for details on facility)

**10% DISCOUNT**
OFF THE PRICE OF YOUR DINNER

ONE VOUCHER PER PERSON

. . . . . . . . . . . . . . . .
Validation

**DO NOT DETACH VOUCHERS FROM THE BOOK**

KISSIMMEE GC FLORIDA

**KISSIMMEE, FL**

(See page 39 for details on facility)

**25% DISCOUNT**

OFF THE CURRENT PRICE OF 18 HOLES WITH CART

VALID ANYTIME
Call ahead for stsrt times

................
Validation

**DO NOT DETACH VOUCHERS FROM THE BOOK**

Lehigh RESORT

**FORT MYERS/LEHIGH, FL**

(See page 41 for details on facility)

**ONE COMPLIMENTARY 18 HOLE ROUND OF GOLF**

when accompanied with one fully paid round of equal value.

NORTH OR SOUTH COURSE
Electric cart rental required
Call ahead for tee times

................
Validation

**DO NOT DETACH VOUCHERS FROM THE BOOK**

PERDIDO BAY

**PENSACOLA, FL**

(See page 45 for details on facility)

**1 COMPLIMENTARY BAG OF RANGE BALLS**

FOR EVERY ROUND OF GOLF

................
Validation

ONE VOUCHER PER PERSON

**DO NOT DETACH VOUCHERS FROM THE BOOK**

Killearn Country Club & Inn

**TALLAHASSEE, FL**

(See page 45 for details on facility)

**1 COMPLIMENTARY BAG OF RANGE BALLS**

FOR EVERY ROUND OF GOLF

................
Validation

ONE VOUCHER PER PERSON

**DO NOT DETACH VOUCHERS FROM THE BOOK**

Plantation Inn and Golf Resort

**CRYSTAL RIVER, FL**

(See page 46 for details on facility)

**10% DISCOUNT**
OFF PRO SHOP MERCHANDISE

ONE VOUCHER PER PERSON
Not valid on gloves or balls

. . . . . . . . . . . . . . . .
Validation

**DO NOT DETACH VOUCHERS FROM THE BOOK**

---

ravines

**MIDDLEBURG, FL**

(See page 47 for details on facility)

**ONE COMPLIMENTARY COCKTAIL**
FOR EACH PERSON STAYING AT THE INN

ONE VOUCHER PER PERSON
Please present upon arrival at the Inn

. . . . . . . . . . . . . . . .
Validation

**DO NOT DETACH VOUCHERS FROM THE BOOK**

---

THE RIVER CLUB

**BRADENTON, FL**

(See page 48 for details on facility)

**1 COMPLIMENTARY BUCKET OF RANGE BALLS**
FOR EVERY ROUND OF 18 HOLES OF GOLF

ONE VOUCHER PER PERSON

. . . . . . . . . . . . . . . .
Validation

**DO NOT DETACH VOUCHERS FROM THE BOOK**

---

ROYAL OAK GOLF CLUB

**TITUSVILLE, FL**

(See page 49 for details on facility)

**ONE 18 HOLE GREEN FEE AND 1/2 CART FOR $12.50 + TAX**
48 HOUR ADVANCED TEE TIME REQUIRED

ONE VOUCHER PER PERSON
Valid May 1 thru October 31, 1992

. . . . . . . . . . . . . . . .
Validation

**DO NOT DETACH VOUCHERS FROM THE BOOK**

**TIMBERWOODS** — *SARASOTA, FL*

(See pages 50 & 51 for details on facility)

**10% DISCOUNT**

OFF SPECIAL GOLF PACKAGES

VALID APRIL 15 TO NOVEMBER 15, 1992

. . . . . . . . . . . . . . . .
Validation

DO NOT DETACH VOUCHERS FROM THE BOOK

---

**TIMACUAN •GOLF AND COUNTRY CLUB•** — *ORLANDO, FL*

(See page 52 for details on facility)

**SPECIAL PRICE - ONLY $30.00**

FOR 18 HOLES AND CART

EXPIRES NOVEMBER 15, 1992
Valid Mon.- Fri. anytime.
Weekends and holidyas after 12:00

. . . . . . . . . . . . . . . .
Validation

DO NOT DETACH VOUCHERS FROM THE BOOK

---

**DAYTONA BEACH HILTON** *The Best on the Beach* — *DAYTONA BEACH, FL*

(See page 56 for details on facility)

**FREE COCKTAIL WITH DINNER**

HOUSE BRANDS ONLY. NO SPECIALTY DRINKS

ONE VOUCHER PER PERSON

. . . . . . . . . . . . . . . .
Validation

DO NOT DETACH VOUCHERS FROM THE BOOK

---

**Perry's OCEAN-EDGE** — *DAYTONA BEACH, FL*

(See page 60 for details on facility)

**FREE GIFT OF YOUR CHOICE**

1 SLEEVE OF PERRY'S GOLF BALLS, OR 1 PERRY'S T-SHIRT,
OR 1 PERRY'S GOLF HAT

ONE GIFT ITEM PER RESERVATION

. . . . . . . . . . . . . . . .
Validation

DO NOT DETACH VOUCHERS FROM THE BOOK

On The Beach

*DAYTONA BEACH, FL*

(See page 33 for details on facility)

**FREE GIFT UPON ARRIVAL**

ONE VOUCHER PER PERSON

................ Validation

DO NOT DETACH VOUCHERS FROM THE BOOK

---

MATANZAS WOODS GOLF CLUB

*PALM COAST, FL*

(See page 63 for details on facility)

**1 COMPLIMENTARY BUCKET OF RANGE BALLS**
FOR EVERY ROUND OF 18 HOLES OF GOLF

ONE VOUCHER PER PERSON

................ Validation

DO NOT DETACH VOUCHERS FROM THE BOOK

---

*PALM COAST, FL*

(See page 63 for details on facility)

**1 COMPLIMENTARY BUCKET OF RANGE BALLS**
FOR EVERY ROUND OF 18 HOLES OF GOLF

ONE VOUCHER PER PERSON

................ Validation

DO NOT DETACH VOUCHERS FROM THE BOOK

---

*PALM COAST, FL*

(See page 63 for details on facility)

**1 COMPLIMENTARY BUCKET OF RANGE BALLS**
FOR EVERY ROUND OF 18 HOLES OF GOLF

ONE VOUCHER PER PERSON

................ Validation

DO NOT DETACH VOUCHERS FROM THE BOOK

## VALUE ADDED VOUCHERS

Palm Harbor Golf Club

**PALM COAST, FL**

(See page 33 for details on facility)

**1 COMPLIMENTARY BUCKET OF RANGE BALLS**
FOR EVERY ROUND OF 18 HOLES OF GOLF

................
Validation

ONE VOUCHER PER PERSON

**DO NOT DETACH VOUCHERS FROM THE BOOK**

The Charter House Inn

**ST. MARY'S, GA**

(See page 66 for details on facility)

**10% DISCOUNT**
IN THE MARKET PLACE RESTAURANT

................
Validation

ONE VOUCHER PER PERSON

**DO NOT DETACH VOUCHERS FROM THE BOOK**

OSPREY COVE

**ST. MARY'S, GA**

(See page 66 for details on facility)

**1 COMPLIMENTARY BUCKET OF RANGE BALLS**
FOR EVERY ROUND OF 18 HOLES OF GOLF

................
Validation

VOUCHER OFFER EXPIRES MAY 30/93

**DO NOT DETACH VOUCHERS FROM THE BOOK**

RAMADA® INN
on Jekyll Island

**JEKYLL ISLAND, GA**

(See page 67 for details on facility)

**2 FREE COCKTAILS IN OUR "MR. HYDE'S" LOUNGE**
WELL BRANDS ONLY

................
Validation

ONE VOUCHER PER PERSON

**DO NOT DETACH VOUCHERS FROM THE BOOK**

CHEBOYGAN, MI

(See page 33 for details on facility)

**$5.00 OFF**

ANY PURCHASE OVER $25.00 IN OUR PROSHOP

. . . . . . . . . . . . . . .
Validation

VOUCHER EXPIRES SEPTEMBER 30/92

**DO NOT DETACH VOUCHERS FROM THE BOOK**

---

LAKEVIEW HILLS C.C. & RESORT — LEXINGTON, MI

(See page78 for details on facility)

**ONE COMPLIMENTARY 9 or 18 HOLE ROUND OF GOLF**

when accompanied with one fully paid round of equal value.

Valid Mon. thru Fri. (except holidays) from 8 a.m. to 12 noon
ON THE SOUTH COURSE ONLY. Power Cart Rental is Required.
Call ahead for assured Tee Times.

. . . . . . . . . . . . . . .
Validation

**DO NOT DETACH VOUCHERS FROM THE BOOK**

---

The Northland Inn & Motel — WATERS, MI

(See page 81 for details on facility)

**10% DISCOUNT**

OFF THE PRICE OF YOUR DINNER

. . . . . . . . . . . . . . .
Validation

ONE VOUCHER PER PERSON
Reservations recommended

**DO NOT DETACH VOUCHERS FROM THE BOOK**

---

POHLCAT — MOUNT PLEASANT, MI

(See page 83 for details on facility)

**1 COMPLIMENTARY BUCKET OF RANGE BALLS**

FOR EVERY ROUND OF 18 HOLES OF GOLF

. . . . . . . . . . . . . . .
Validation

ONE VOUCHER PER PERSON

**DO NOT DETACH VOUCHERS FROM THE BOOK**

# VALUE ADDED VOUCHERS

TAWAS GOLF COURSE

***TAWAS, MI***

(See page 87 for details on facility)

**ONE COMPLIMENTARY 9 or 18 HOLE ROUND OF GOLF**
when accompanied with one fully paid round of equal value.

VAILID MON. THRU THURS. (except holidays) 11 to 2.
VALID WEEKENDS AND HOLIDYAS AFTER 4.
Power Cart Rental is Required.
Call ahead for assured Tee Times.

. . . . . . . . . . . . . . . .
Validation

**DO NOT DETACH VOUCHERS FROM THE BOOK**

---

EDGEWATER INN

***BILOXI, MS***

(See page 90 for details on facility)

**$5.00 DISCOUNT**
OFF YOUR ROOM RATE

. . . . . . . . . . . . . . . .
Validation

ONE VOUCHER PER PERSON/PER ROOM

**DO NOT DETACH VOUCHERS FROM THE BOOK**

---

Pine island Golf Course

***OCEAN SPRINGS, MS***

(See page 91 for details on facility)

**20% DISCOUNT**
ON GREEN FEES

. . . . . . . . . . . . . . . .
Validation

VOUCHER VALID FROM May1/92 TO Jan. 31/93

**DO NOT DETACH VOUCHERS FROM THE BOOK**

---

St. Andrews ON THE GULF

***OCEAN SPRINGS, MS***

(See page 91 for details on facility)

**20% DISCOUNT**
ON GREEN FEES

. . . . . . . . . . . . . . . .
Validation

VOUCHER VALID FROM May1/92 TO Jan. 31/93

**DO NOT DETACH VOUCHERS FROM THE BOOK**

SHONEY'S INN

***GULFPORT, MS***

(See page 96 for details on facility)

**5% DISCOUNT**
OFF GOLF PACKAGES

ONE VOUCHER PER PERSON
Per person - Double occupancy
Not valid with any other discount

................
Validation

**DO NOT DETACH VOUCHERS FROM THE BOOK**

BLUE HERON HILLS
Country Club

***MACEDON, NY***

(See page 97 for details on facility)

**1 COMPLIMENTARY BUCKET OF RANGE BALLS**
FOR EVERY ROUND OF 18 HOLES OF GOLF

................
Validation

ONE VOUCHER PER PERSON

**DO NOT DETACH VOUCHERS FROM THE BOOK**

TERRY HILLS

***BATAVIA, NY***

(See page 100 for details on facility)

**ONE COMPLIMENTARY ROUND OF GOLF**
when accompanied with one fully paid round of equal value.

VALID MON. THRU FRI.
Power Cart Rental is Required.
Tee times required 24 hours in advance.

................
Validation

**DO NOT DETACH VOUCHERS FROM THE BOOK**

Peek'n Peak

***CLYMER, NY***

(See page 102 for details on facility)

**15% DISCOUNT**
OFF WEEKDAY GOLF

ONE VOUCHER PER PERSON
Valid Mon. thru Thurs.
May 1/92 to October 31/92

................
Validation

**DO NOT DETACH VOUCHERS FROM THE BOOK**

Cypress Lakes

**HOPE MILLS, NC**

(See page 105 for details on facility)

**1 COMPLIMENTARY BUCKET OF RANGE BALLS**
FOR EVERY ROUND OF 18 HOLES OF GOLF

ONE VOUCHER PER PERSON
Voucher expires March 31, 1993

. . . . . . . . . . . . . . . . .
Validation

**DO NOT DETACH VOUCHERS FROM THE BOOK**

---

Holiday Inn

**BURLINGTON, NC**

(See page 108 for details on facility)

**1 COMPLIMENTARY SLEEVE OF GOLF BALLS**
WHEN YOU CHOOSE ANY OF OUR GOLF PACKAGES

. . . . . . . . . . . . . . . . .
Validation

ONE VOUCHER PER PERSON

**DO NOT DETACH VOUCHERS FROM THE BOOK**

---

**NAGS HEAD**
**GOLF LINKS**

**NAGS HEAD, NC**

(See page 111 for details on facility)

**1 COMPLIMENTARY BUCKET OF RANGE BALLS**
FOR EVERY ROUND OF 18 HOLES OF GOLF

. . . . . . . . . . . . . . . . .
Validation

ONE VOUCHER PER PERSON

**DO NOT DETACH VOUCHERS FROM THE BOOK**

---

Beacon Ridge

**WEST END, NC**

(See page 114 for details on facility)

**BRING A FOURSOME - PAY FOR THREE**
FOR UP TO $80.00 IN SAVINGS

ONE VOUCHER PER FOURSOME
Call for more information and details

. . . . . . . . . . . . . . . . .
Validation

**DO NOT DETACH VOUCHERS FROM THE BOOK**

FOXFIRE Resort & Country Club

***PINEHURST, NC***

(See page 115 for details on facility)

**ONE COMPLIMENTARY ROUND OF GOLF**

when accompanied with one fully paid round of equal value.

VALID NOV. 16/92 TO MARCH 15/93
Power Cart Rental is Required.
Tee times required 24 hours in advance.

Validation

DO NOT DETACH VOUCHERS FROM THE BOOK

Hampton Inn

***SOUTHERN PINES/PINEHURST, NC***

(See page 116 for details on facility)

**20% DISCOUNT**

OFF YOUR ROOM RATE

ONE VOUCHER PER PERSON
Reservations required 2 weeks in advance
Valid July-Aug. 1992 / Nov.-Dec. 1992

Validation

DO NOT DETACH VOUCHERS FROM THE BOOK

Hyland Hills GOLF CLUB

***SOUTHERN PINES, NC***

(See page 177 for details on facility)

**10% DISCOUNT**

OFF GREEN FEES

ONE VOUCHER PER PERSON

Validation

DO NOT DETACH VOUCHERS FROM THE BOOK

Beau Rivage Plantation

***WILMINGTON, NC***

(See page 121 for details on facility)

**FREE LOGO GOLF BALL**

ONE VOUCHER PER PERSON

Validation

DO NOT DETACH VOUCHERS FROM THE BOOK

The Cape
GOLF & RACQUET CLUB INC.

**WILMINGTON, NC**

(See page 122 for details on facility)

**1 COMPLIMENTARY BUCKET OF RANGE BALLS**
FOR EVERY ROUND OF 18 HOLES OF GOLF

................ Validation

ONE VOUCHER PER PERSON

**DO NOT DETACH VOUCHERS FROM THE BOOK**

---

Fox Squirrel
Country Club

**SOUTHPORT, NC**

(See page 33 for details on facility)

**20% OFF ALL CLUBS & BAGS**
**25% OFF ALL OTHER CLOTHING ITEMS**

................ Validation

VOUCHER EXPIRES MAY 31/93

**DO NOT DETACH VOUCHERS FROM THE BOOK**

---

PORTERS NECK PLANTATION
AND COUNTRY CLUB

**WILMINGTON, NC**

(See page 125 for details on facility)

**1 COMPLIMENTARY BUCKET OF RANGE BALLS**
FOR EVERY ROUND OF 18 HOLES OF GOLF

................ Validation

VOUCHER EXPIRES DECEMBER 31/92

**DO NOT DETACH VOUCHERS FROM THE BOOK**

---

CHARLESTON NATIONAL

**MT. PLEASANT, SC**

(See page 33 for details on facility)

**$6.00 OFF GREEN FEES**

................ Validation

ONE VOUCHER PER PERSON

**DO NOT DETACH VOUCHERS FROM THE BOOK**

The Phil Ritson Golf School

***PAWLEYS ISLAND, SC***

(See page 140 for details on facility)

**10% DISCOUNT**

ON ANY 3 OR 5 DAY GOLF SCHOOL

................

VOUCHER VALID THRU FEBRUARY 28 1993

Validation

DO NOT DETACH VOUCHERS FROM THE BOOK

---

Old South Golf Links

***HILTON HEAD, SC***

(See page 145 for details on facility)

**25% OFF GREEN FEES ANYTIME**

................

Validation

ONE VOUCHER PER PERSON

DO NOT DETACH VOUCHERS FROM THE BOOK

---

ROSE HILL COUNTRY CLUB

***HILTON HEAD, SC***

(See page 150 for details on facility)

**1 COMPLIMENTARY BAG OF RANGE BALLS**

FOR EVERY 18 HOLES OF GOLF

................

Validation

ONE VOUCHER PER PERSON

DO NOT DETACH VOUCHERS FROM THE BOOK

---

Bryce

***BASYE, VA***

(See page 178 for details on facility)

**$2.00 OFF GREEN FEES**

................

VOUCHER EXPIRES DECEMBER 31/1992

Validation

DO NOT DETACH VOUCHERS FROM THE BOOK

KILN CREEK Golf and Country Club

***NEWPORT NEWS, VA***

(See page 180 for details on facility)

**$10.00 OFF GREEN FEES**

VOUCHER EXPIRES AUG. 31/1992
Valid Monday to Friday

. . . . . . . . . . . . . . . .
Validation

**DO NOT DETACH VOUCHERS FROM THE BOOK**

# ALPHABETICAL INDEX

## *ALPHABETICAL INDEX*

..HONEY WHAT'LL WE DO ON OUR VACATION THIS YEAR??
..I DUNNO, I KEEP THINKING ABOUT IT!...
GOLF VACATION IN CANADA
GOLF IN EUROPE
GOLF IN NEW ZEALAND
GOLF GOLF GOLF
GOLF
Al Kowtz